Y0-AGH-792

HELP STAMP
OUT GRAPES

by
Johnny Hart and Brant Parker

A FAWCETT GOLD MEDAL BOOK · NEW YORK

HELP STAMP OUT GRAPES

© 1973 Publishers Newspaper Syndicate

© 1978 CBS Publications, The Consumer Publishing Division of CBS Inc.

All rights reserved

A Fawcett Gold Medal Book published by special arrangement with Field Newspaper Syndicate.

ISBN 0-449-13992-1

Printed in the United States of America

10   9   8   7   6   5   4   3   2

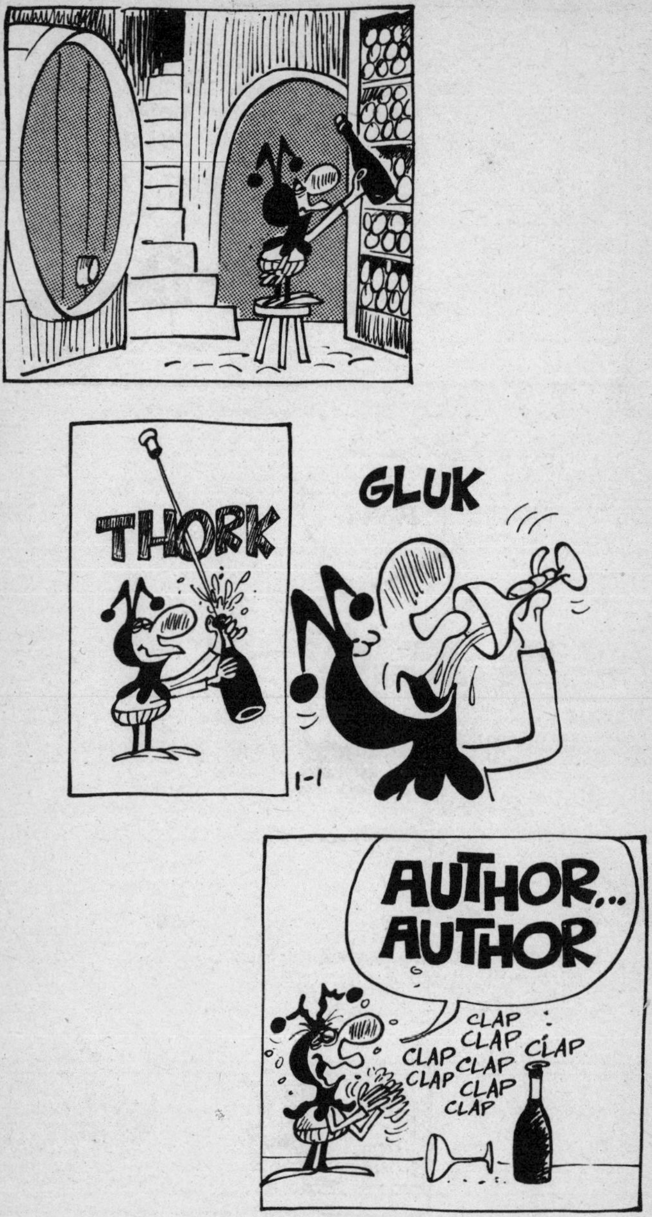
THORK
GLUK
1-1
AUTHOR,... AUTHOR
CLAP CLAP
CLAP CLAP CLAP CLAP CLAP
CLAP
CLAP

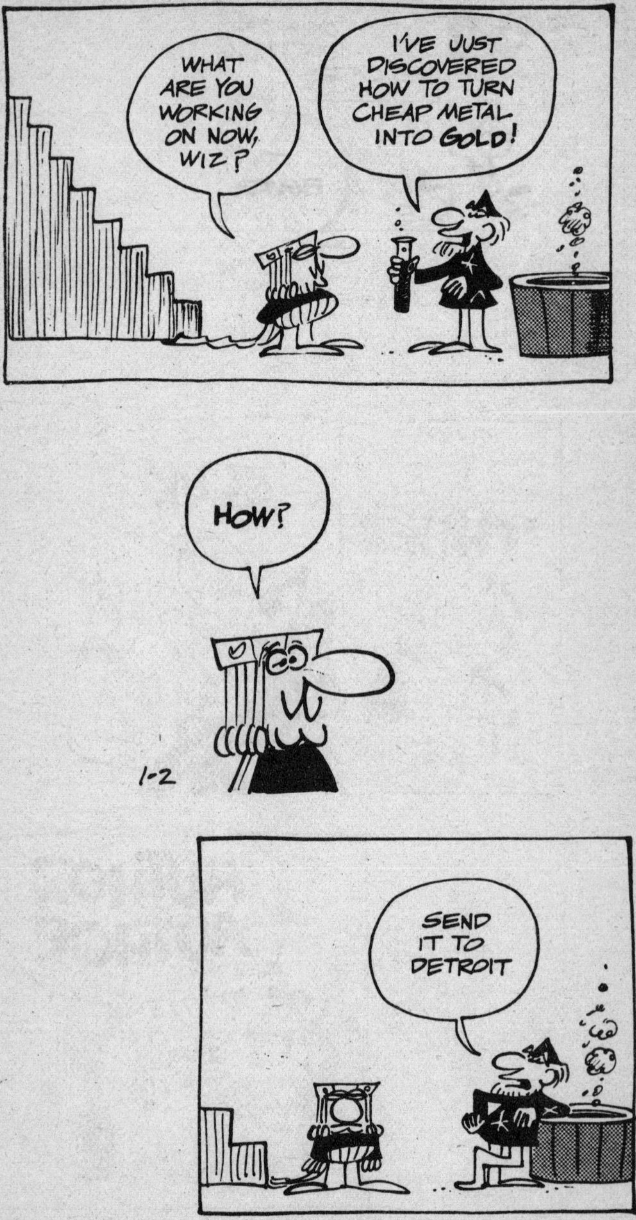
WHAT ARE YOU WORKING ON NOW, WIZ?
I'VE JUST DISCOVERED HOW TO TURN CHEAP METAL INTO GOLD!
HOW?
1-2
SEND IT TO DETROIT

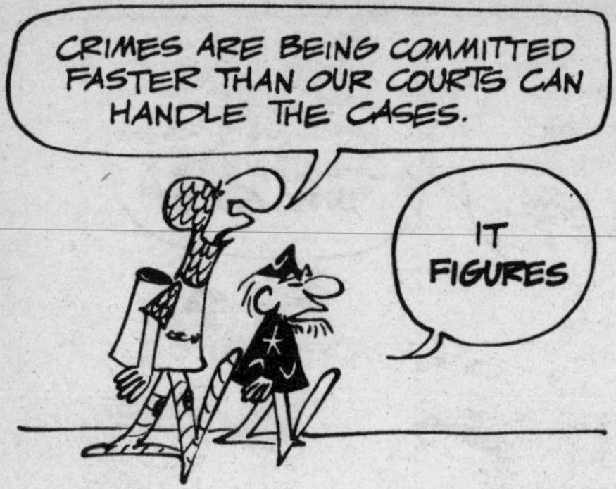
CRIMES ARE BEING COMMITTED FASTER THAN OUR COURTS CAN HANDLE THE CASES.
IT FIGURES

1-3

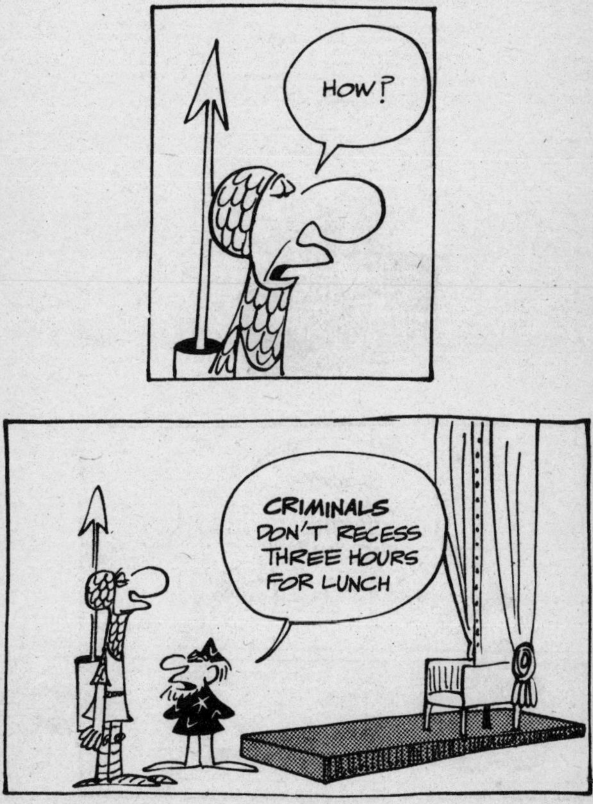
HOW?
CRIMINALS DON'T RECESS THREE HOURS FOR LUNCH

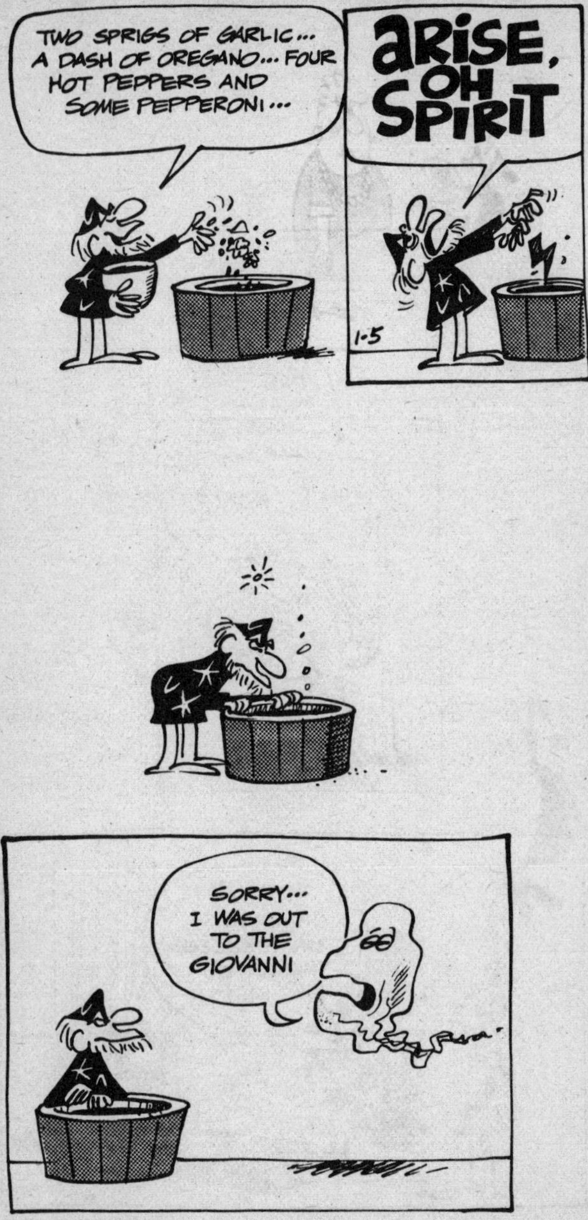
TWO SPRIGS OF GARLIC... A DASH OF OREGANO... FOUR HOT PEPPERS AND SOME PEPPERONI...
ARISE, OH SPIRIT
1-5
SORRY... I WAS OUT TO THE GIOVANNI

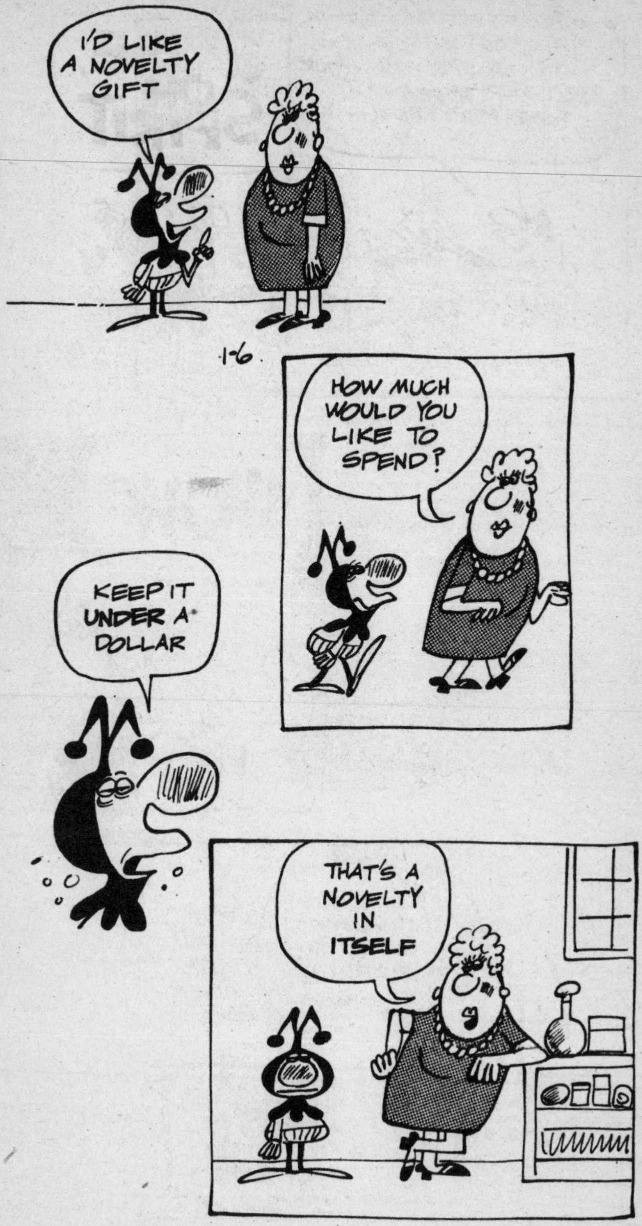
I'D LIKE A NOVELTY GIFT
1-6
HOW MUCH WOULD YOU LIKE TO SPEND?
KEEP IT UNDER A DOLLAR
THAT'S A NOVELTY IN ITSELF

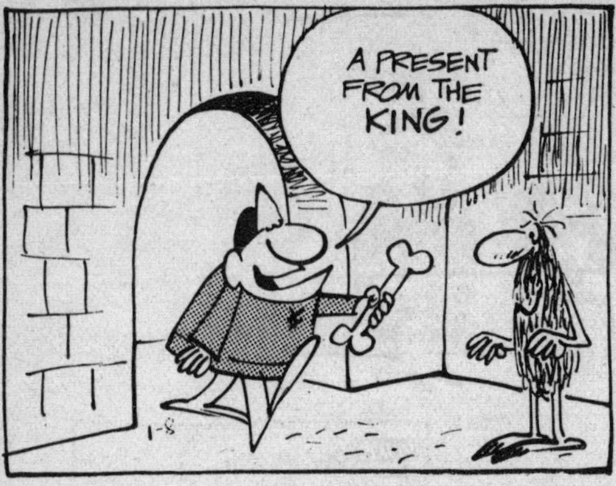
A PRESENT FROM THE KING!
1-8

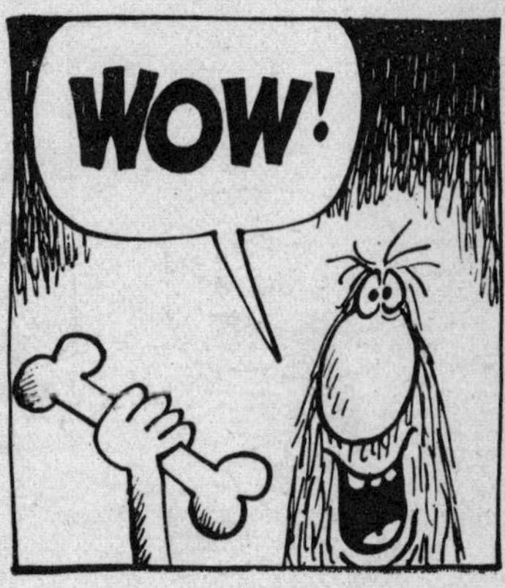
WOW!

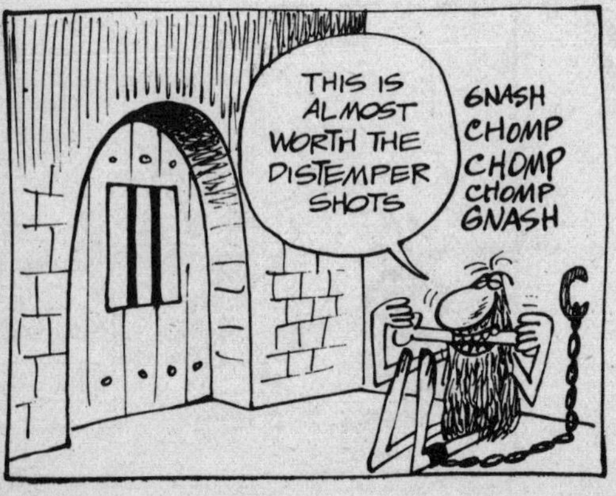
THIS IS ALMOST WORTH THE DISTEMPER SHOTS
GNASH CHOMP CHOMP CHOMP GNASH

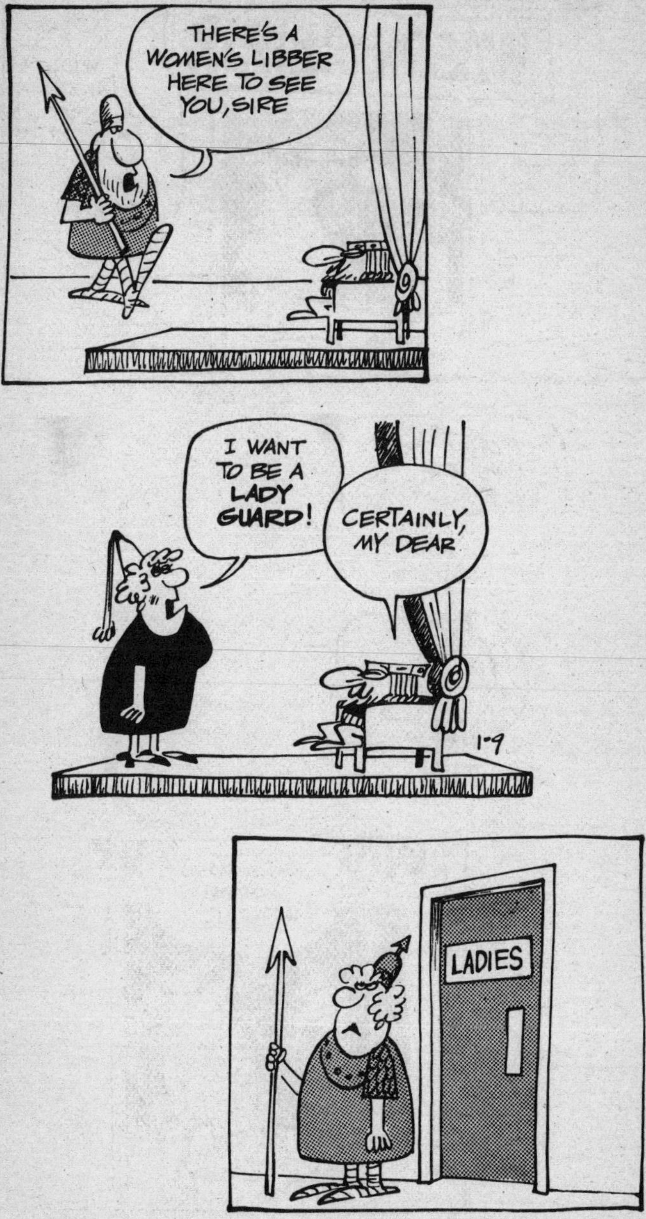
THERE'S A WOMEN'S LIBBER HERE TO SEE YOU, SIRE
I WANT TO BE A LADY GUARD!
CERTAINLY, MY DEAR
1-9
LADIES

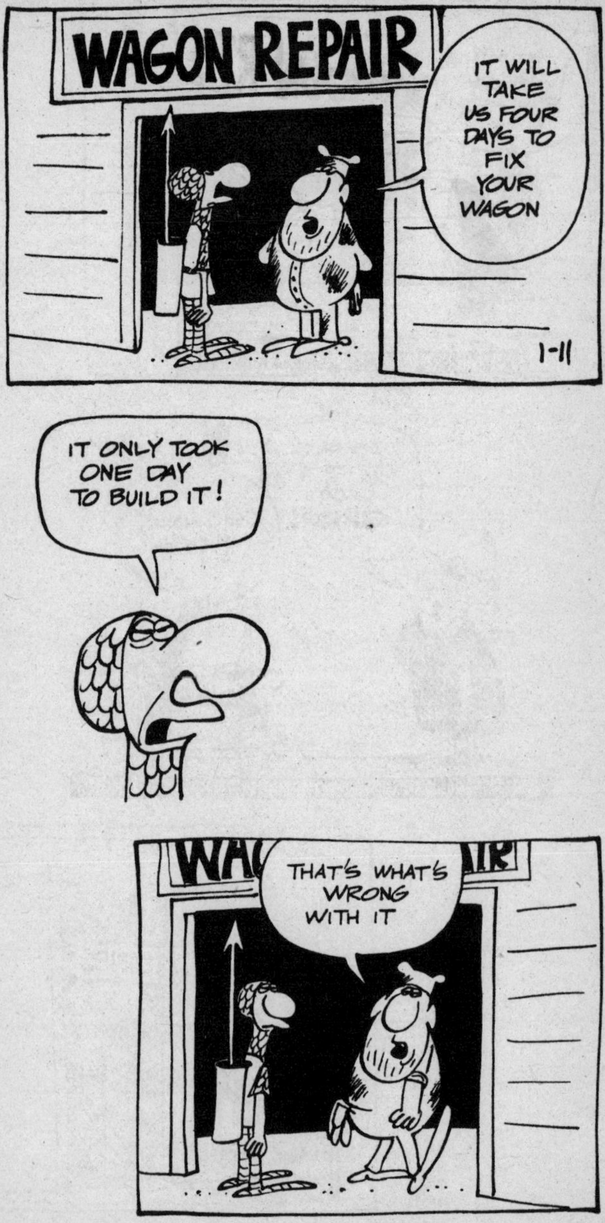
WAGON REPAIR
IT WILL TAKE US FOUR DAYS TO FIX YOUR WAGON
1-11
IT ONLY TOOK ONE DAY TO BUILD IT!
THAT'S WHAT'S WRONG WITH IT

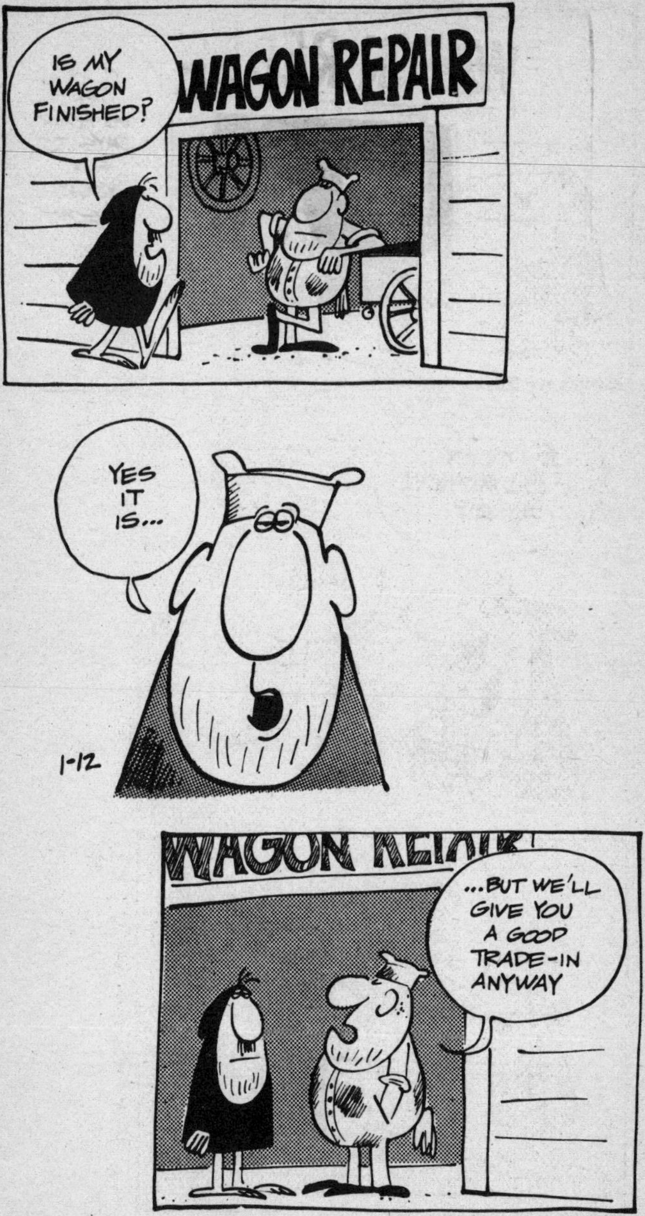
IS MY WAGON FINISHED?
WAGON REPAIR
YES IT IS...
1-12
...BUT WE'LL GIVE YOU A GOOD TRADE-IN ANYWAY

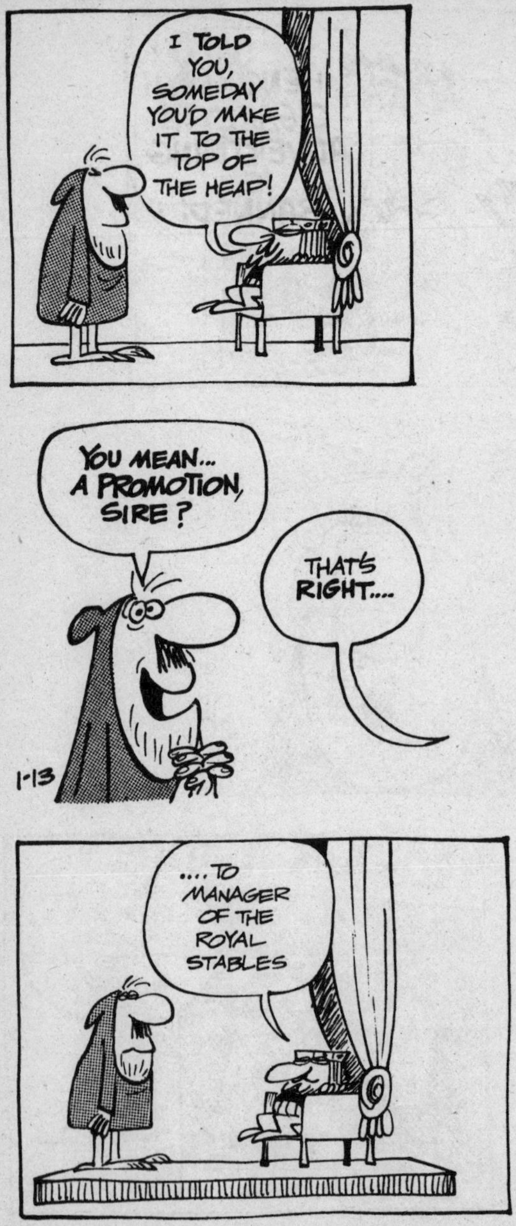
I TOLD YOU, SOMEDAY YOU'D MAKE IT TO THE TOP OF THE HEAP!
YOU MEAN... A PROMOTION, SIRE?
THAT'S RIGHT....
1-13
....TO MANAGER OF THE ROYAL STABLES

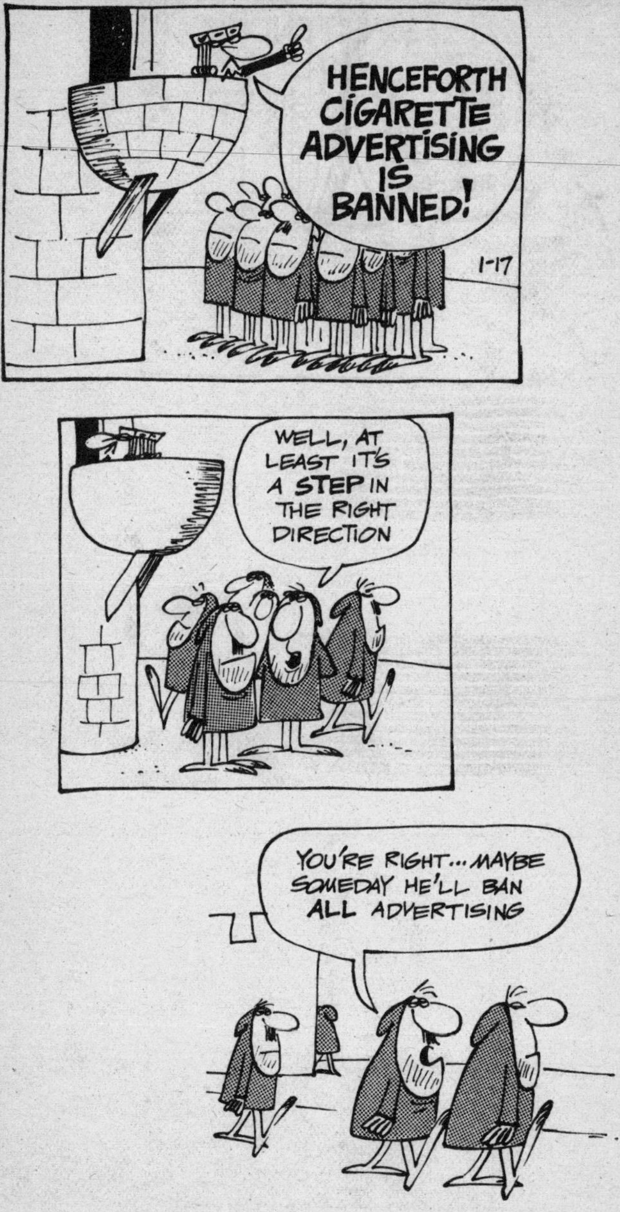
HENCEFORTH CIGARETTE ADVERTISING IS BANNED!
1-17
WELL, AT LEAST IT'S A STEP IN THE RIGHT DIRECTION
YOU'RE RIGHT... MAYBE SOMEDAY HE'LL BAN ALL ADVERTISING

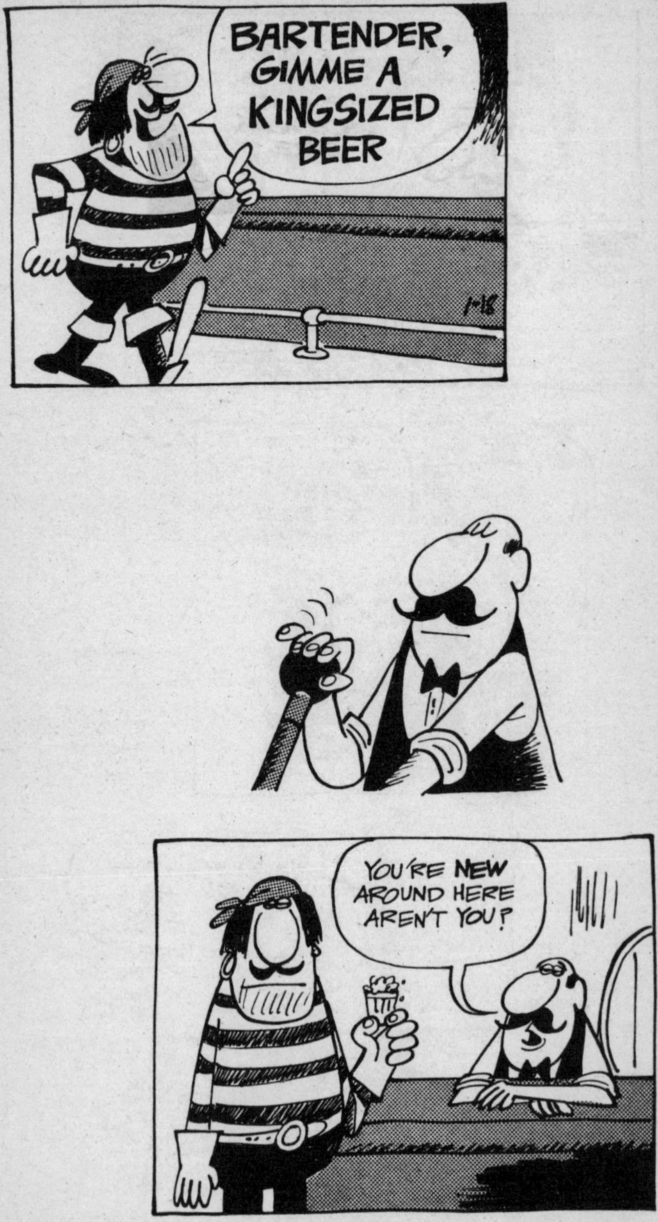
BARTENDER, GIMME A KINGSIZED BEER
YOU'RE NEW AROUND HERE AREN'T YOU?

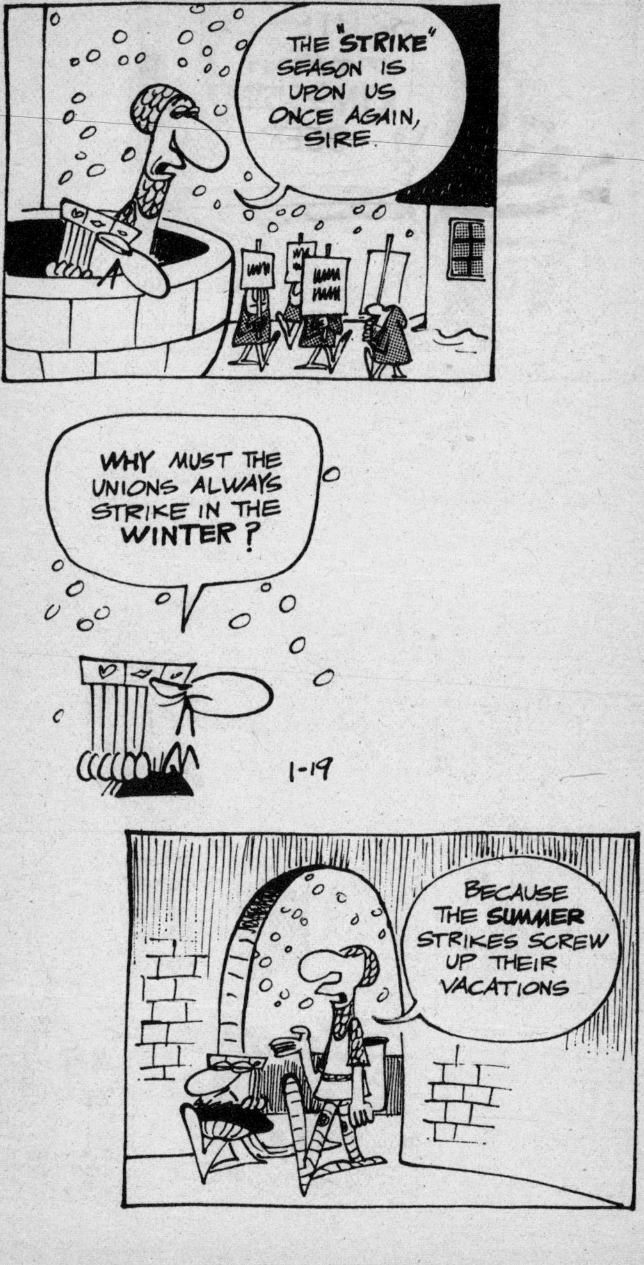
THE "STRIKE" SEASON IS UPON US ONCE AGAIN, SIRE.
WHY MUST THE UNIONS ALWAYS STRIKE IN THE WINTER?
1-19
BECAUSE THE SUMMER STRIKES SCREW UP THEIR VACATIONS

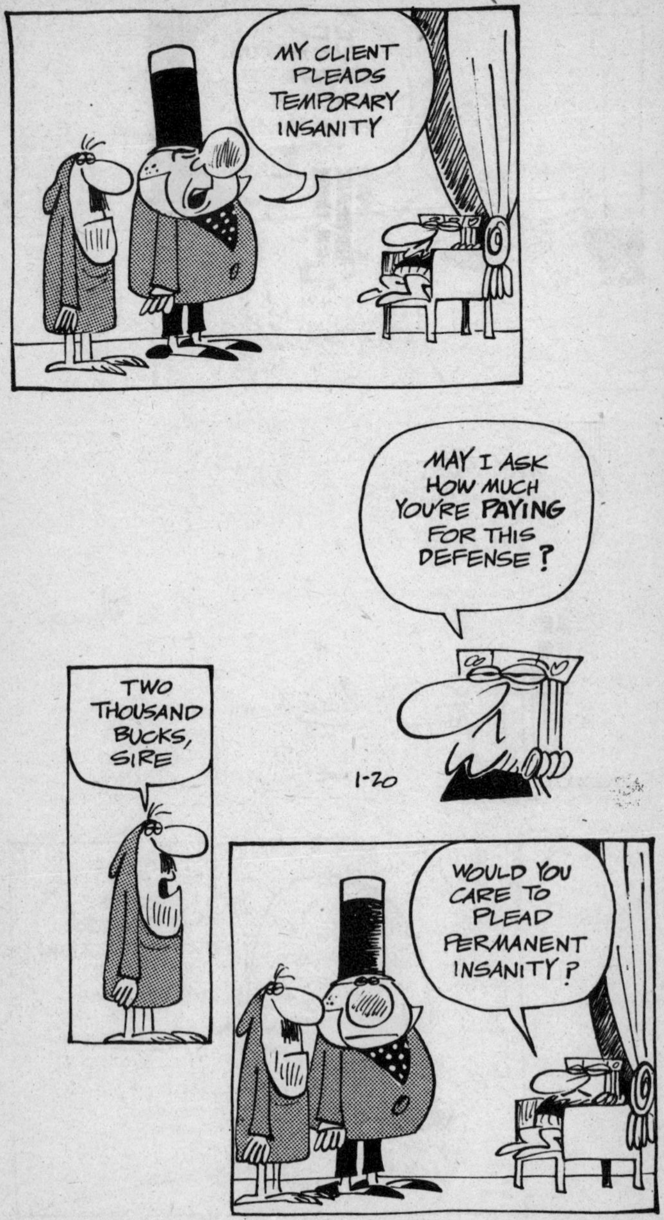
MY CLIENT PLEADS TEMPORARY INSANITY
MAY I ASK HOW MUCH YOU'RE PAYING FOR THIS DEFENSE?
TWO THOUSAND BUCKS, SIRE
1-20
WOULD YOU CARE TO PLEAD PERMANENT INSANITY?

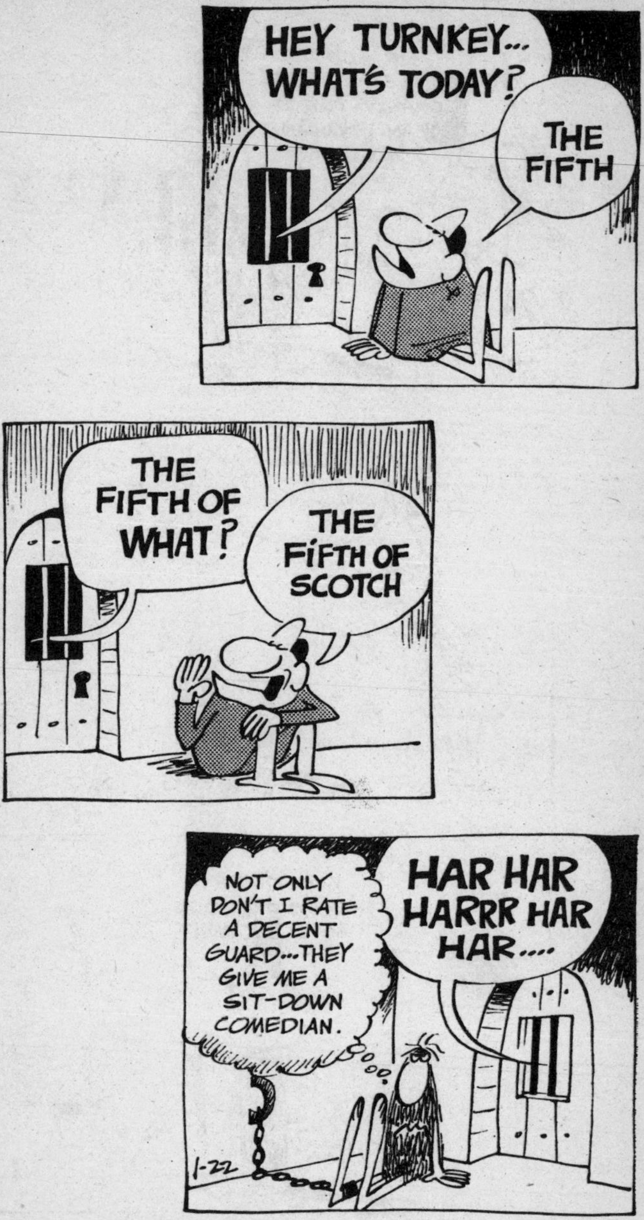
HEY TURNKEY... WHAT'S TODAY?
THE FIFTH
THE FIFTH OF WHAT?
THE FIFTH OF SCOTCH
NOT ONLY DON'T I RATE A DECENT GUARD...THEY GIVE ME A SIT-DOWN COMEDIAN.
HAR HAR HARRR HAR HAR....
1-22

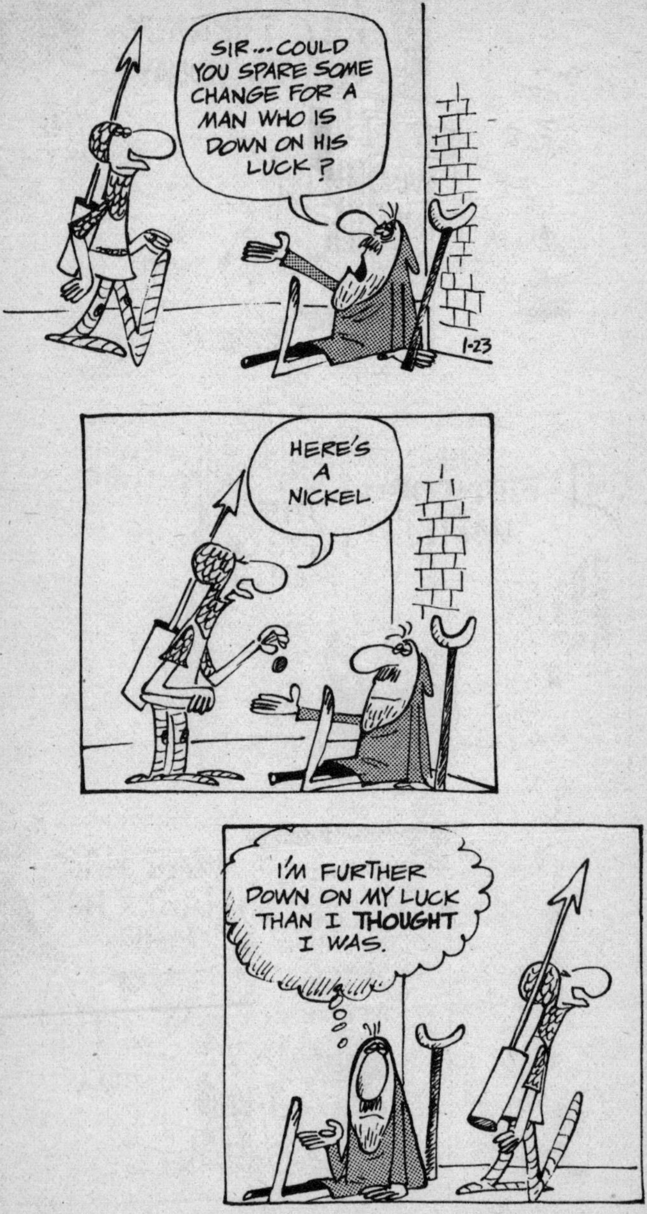
SIR... COULD YOU SPARE SOME CHANGE FOR A MAN WHO IS DOWN ON HIS LUCK?
1-23
HERE'S A NICKEL.
I'M FURTHER DOWN ON MY LUCK THAN I THOUGHT I WAS.

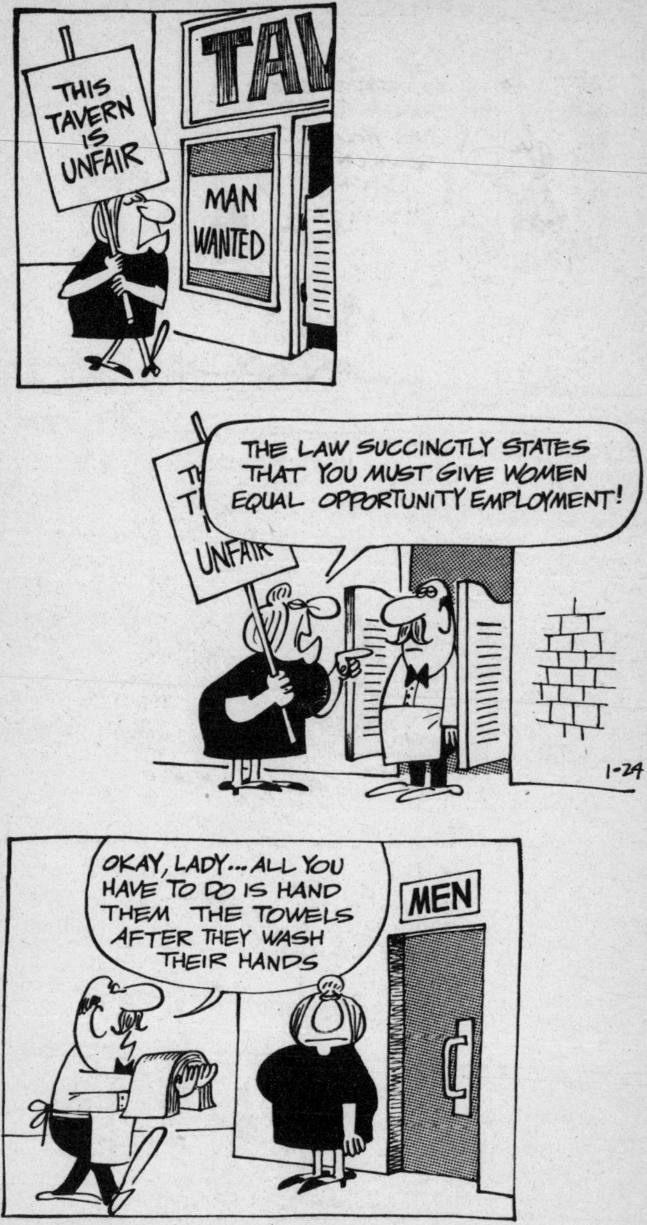
THIS TAVERN IS UNFAIR
TAV
MAN WANTED
THE LAW SUCCINCTLY STATES THAT YOU MUST GIVE WOMEN EQUAL OPPORTUNITY EMPLOYMENT!
UNFAIR
1-24
OKAY, LADY... ALL YOU HAVE TO DO IS HAND THEM THE TOWELS AFTER THEY WASH THEIR HANDS
MEN

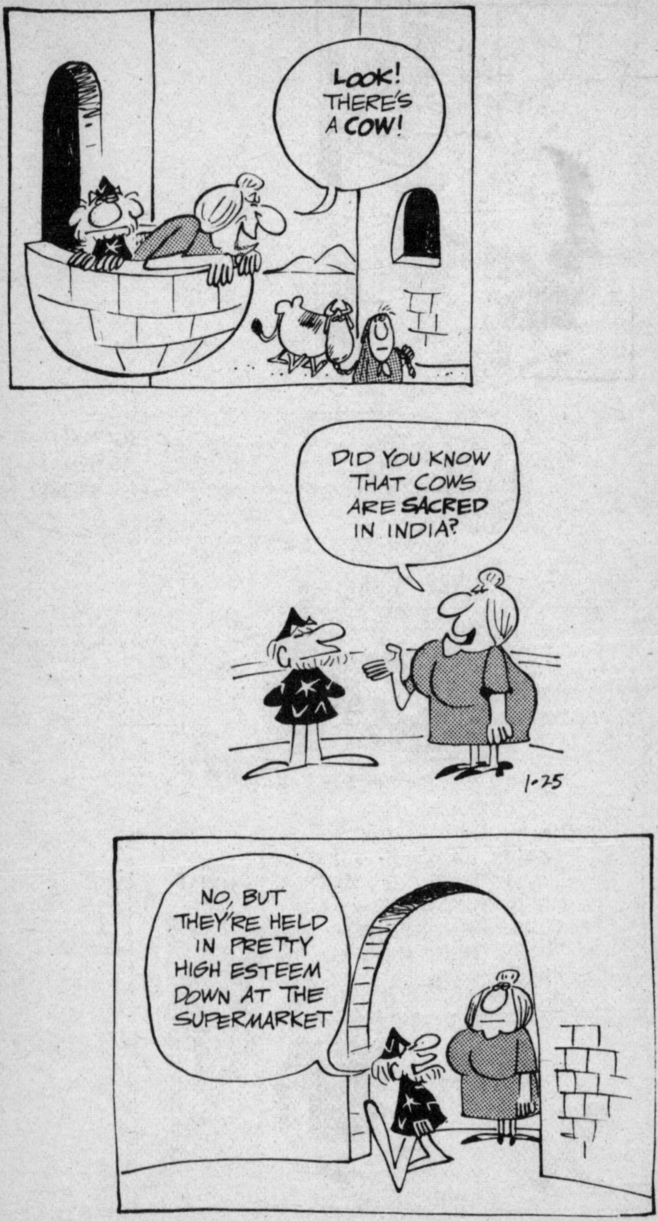
LOOK! THERE'S A COW!
DID YOU KNOW THAT COWS ARE SACRED IN INDIA?
1-25
NO, BUT THEY'RE HELD IN PRETTY HIGH ESTEEM DOWN AT THE SUPERMARKET

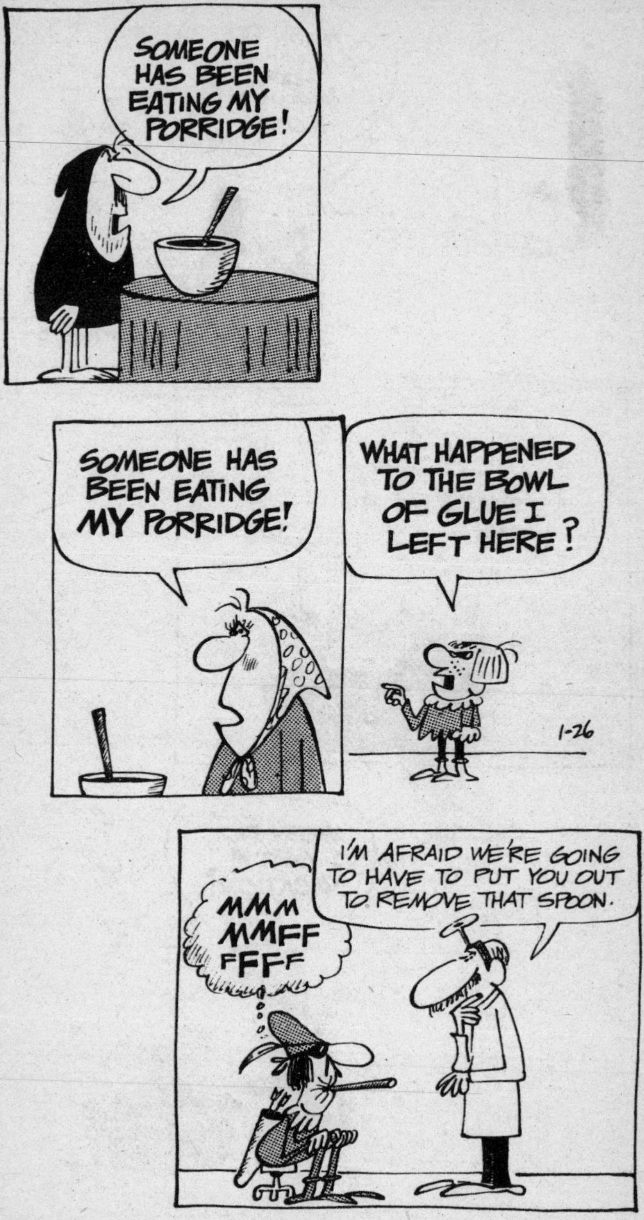

SOMEONE HAS BEEN EATING MY PORRIDGE!
SOMEONE HAS BEEN EATING MY PORRIDGE!
WHAT HAPPENED TO THE BOWL OF GLUE I LEFT HERE?
1-26
MMMM MMFF FFFF
I'M AFRAID WE'RE GOING TO HAVE TO PUT YOU OUT TO REMOVE THAT SPOON.

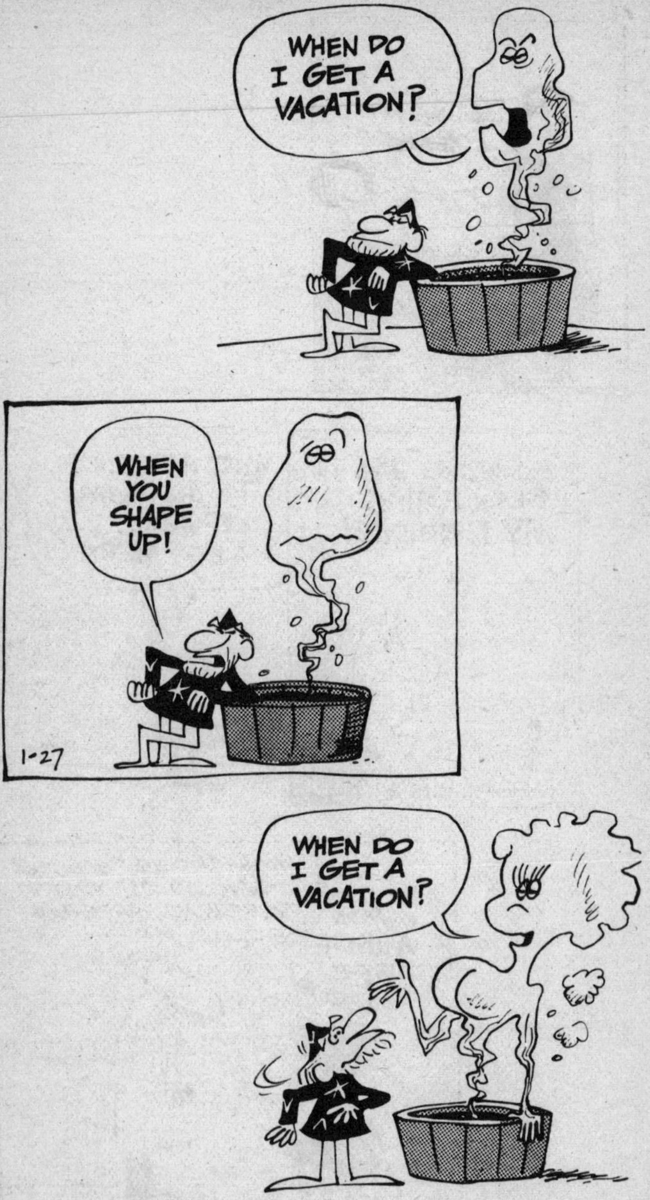
WHEN DO I GET A VACATION?
WHEN YOU SHAPE UP!
1-27
WHEN DO I GET A VACATION?

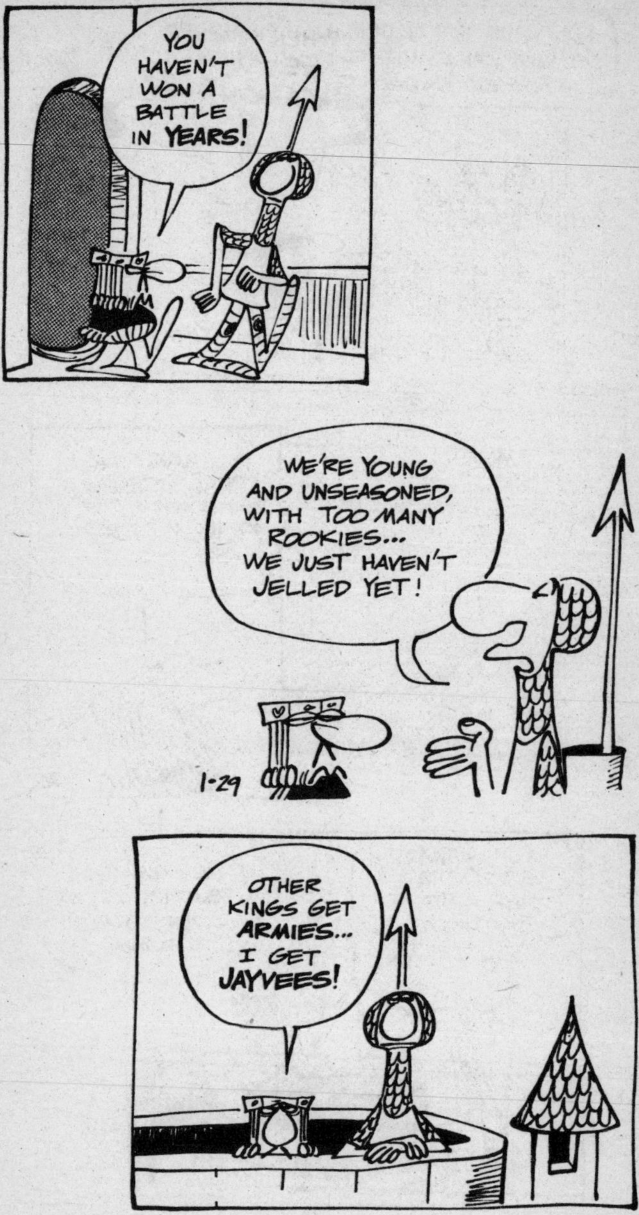
YOU HAVEN'T WON A BATTLE IN YEARS!
WE'RE YOUNG AND UNSEASONED, WITH TOO MANY ROOKIES... WE JUST HAVEN'T JELLED YET!
1-29
OTHER KINGS GET ARMIES... I GET JAYVEES!

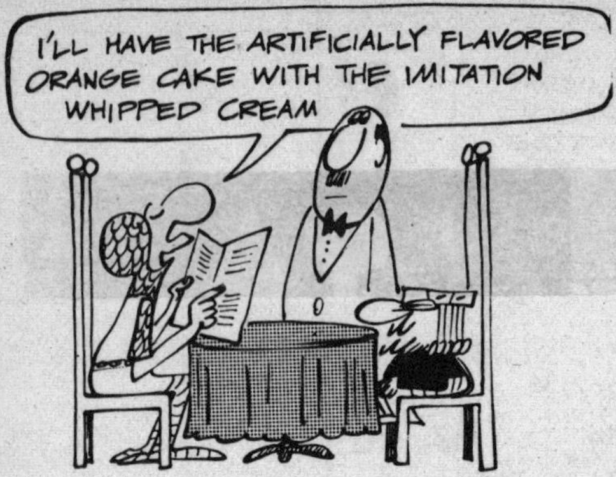
I'LL HAVE THE ARTIFICIALLY FLAVORED ORANGE CAKE WITH THE IMITATION WHIPPED CREAM

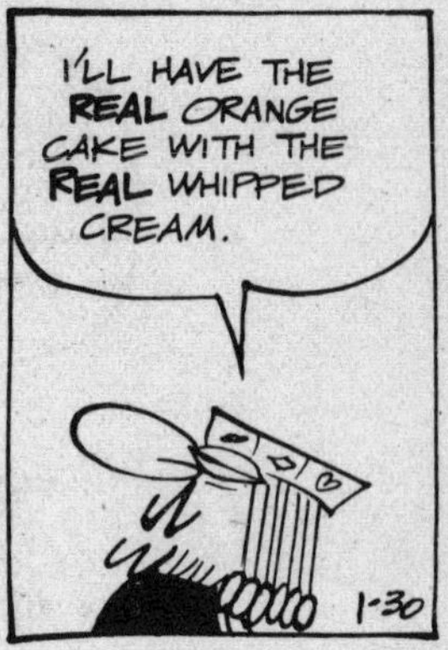
I'LL HAVE THE REAL ORANGE CAKE WITH THE REAL WHIPPED CREAM.
1-30

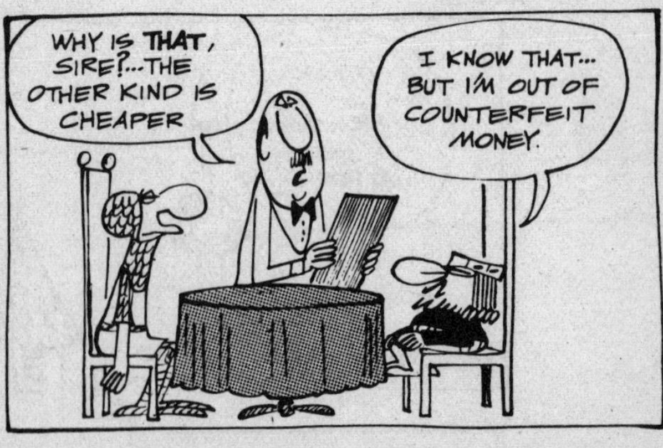
WHY IS THAT, SIRE?...THE OTHER KIND IS CHEAPER
I KNOW THAT... BUT I'M OUT OF COUNTERFEIT MONEY.

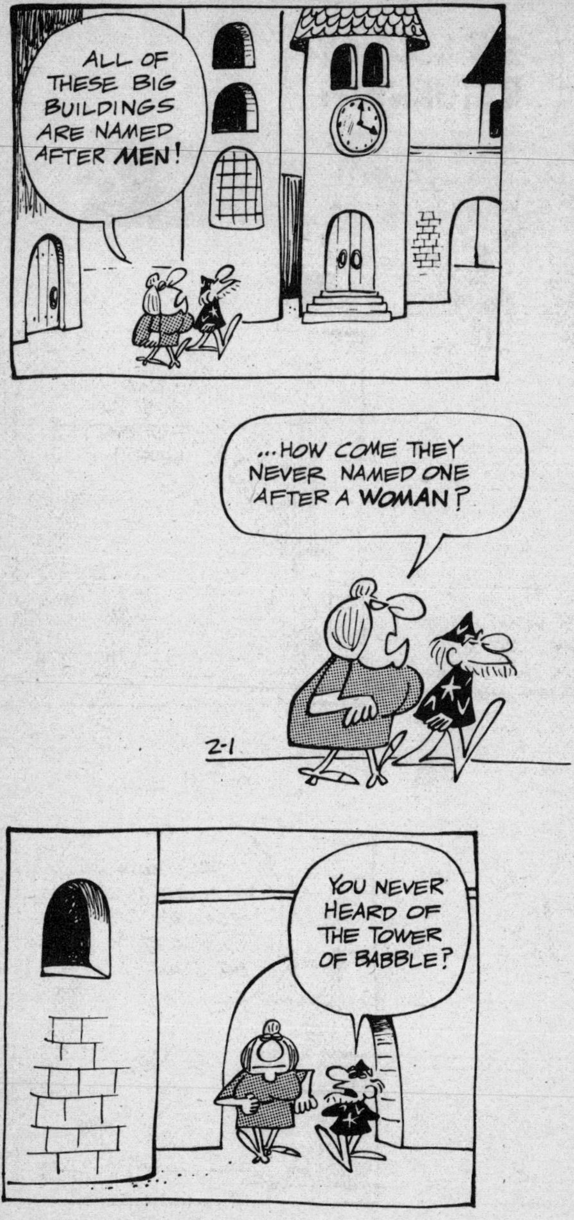
ALL OF THESE BIG BUILDINGS ARE NAMED AFTER MEN!
...HOW COME THEY NEVER NAMED ONE AFTER A WOMAN?
2-1
YOU NEVER HEARD OF THE TOWER OF BABBLE?

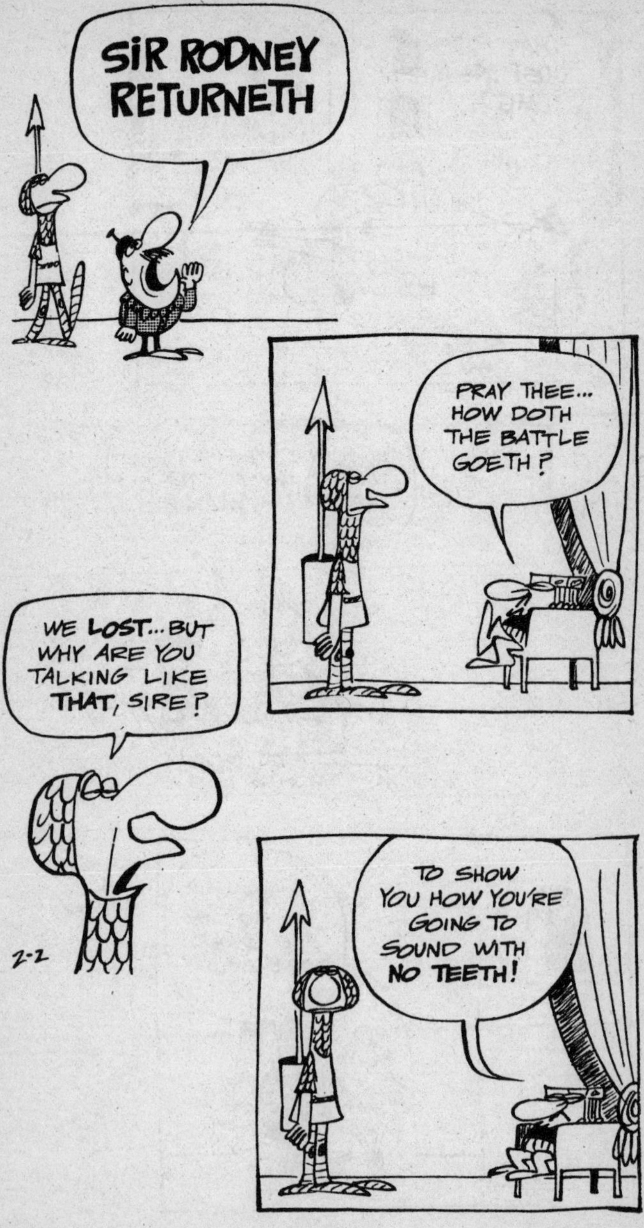

SIR RODNEY RETURNETH
PRAY THEE... HOW DOTH THE BATTLE GOETH?
WE LOST... BUT WHY ARE YOU TALKING LIKE THAT, SIRE?
2-2
TO SHOW YOU HOW YOU'RE GOING TO SOUND WITH NO TEETH!

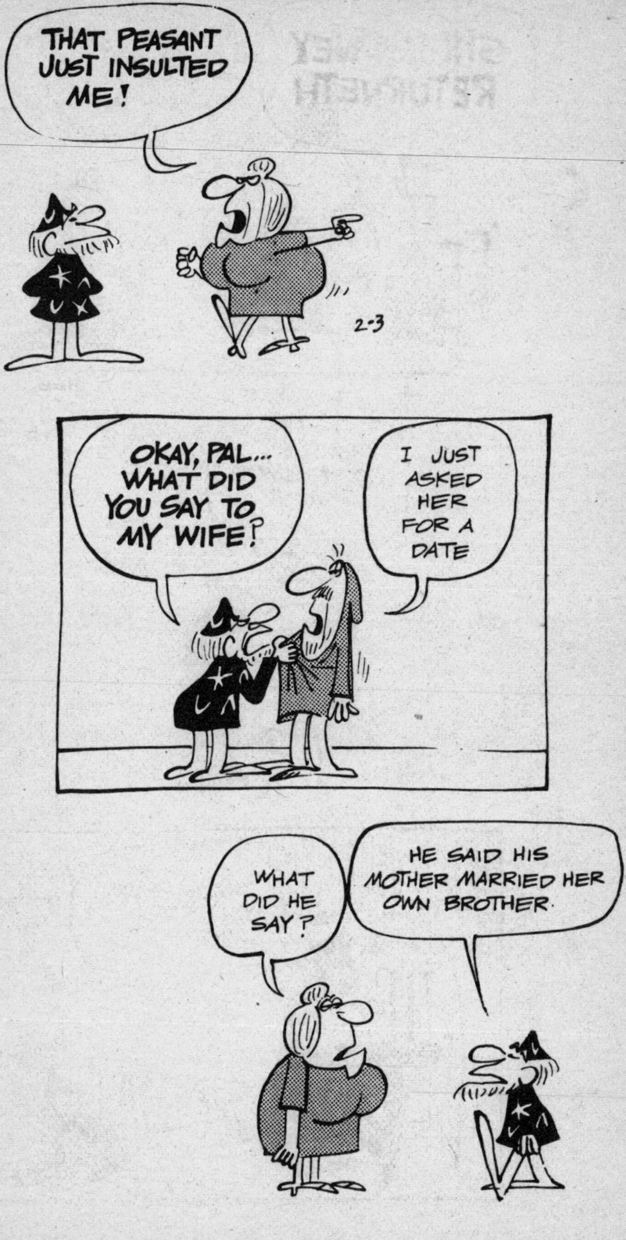
THAT PEASANT JUST INSULTED ME!
2-3
OKAY, PAL... WHAT DID YOU SAY TO MY WIFE?
I JUST ASKED HER FOR A DATE
WHAT DID HE SAY?
HE SAID HIS MOTHER MARRIED HER OWN BROTHER.

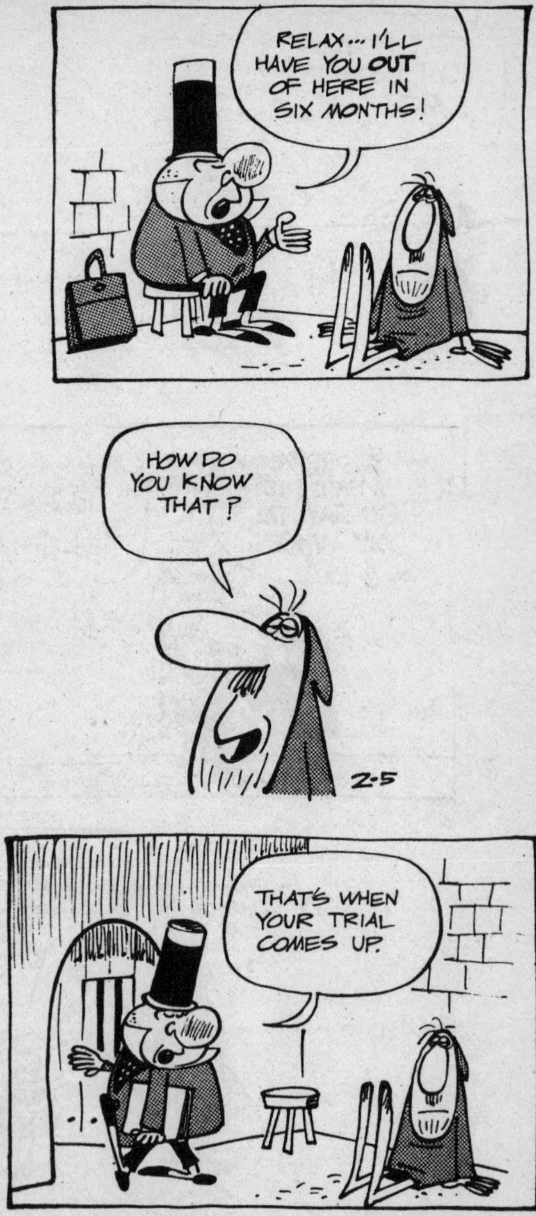
RELAX... I'LL HAVE YOU OUT OF HERE IN SIX MONTHS!
HOW DO YOU KNOW THAT?
2-5
THAT'S WHEN YOUR TRIAL COMES UP.

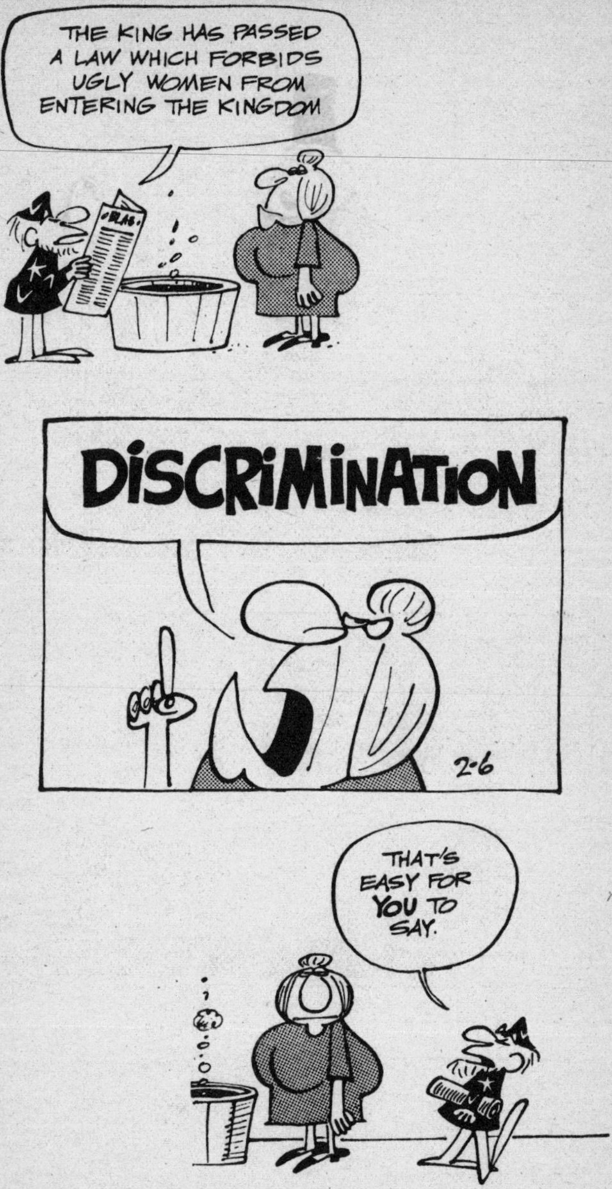
THE KING HAS PASSED A LAW WHICH FORBIDS UGLY WOMEN FROM ENTERING THE KINGDOM
BLAB
DISCRIMINATION
2-6
THAT'S EASY FOR YOU TO SAY.

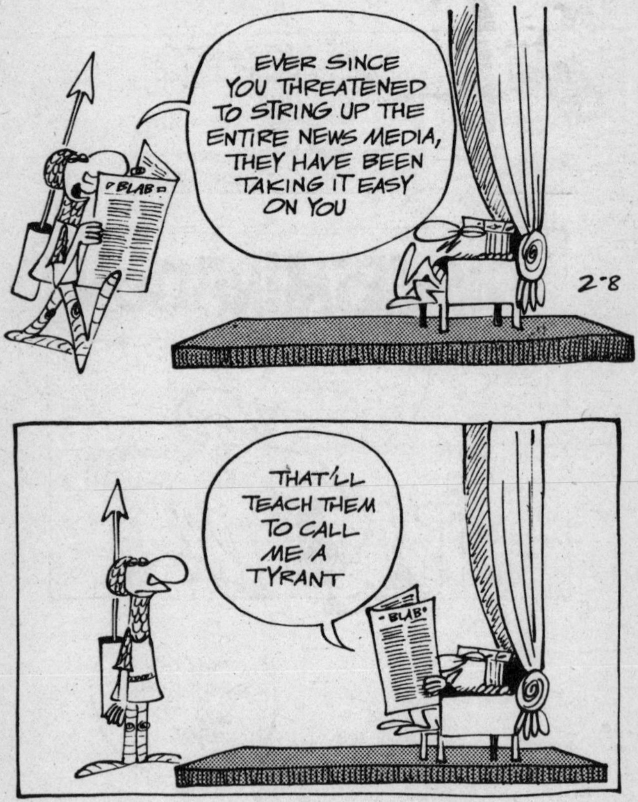
EVER SINCE YOU THREATENED TO STRING UP THE ENTIRE NEWS MEDIA, THEY HAVE BEEN TAKING IT EASY ON YOU
BLAB
2-8
THAT'LL TEACH THEM TO CALL ME A TYRANT
BLAB

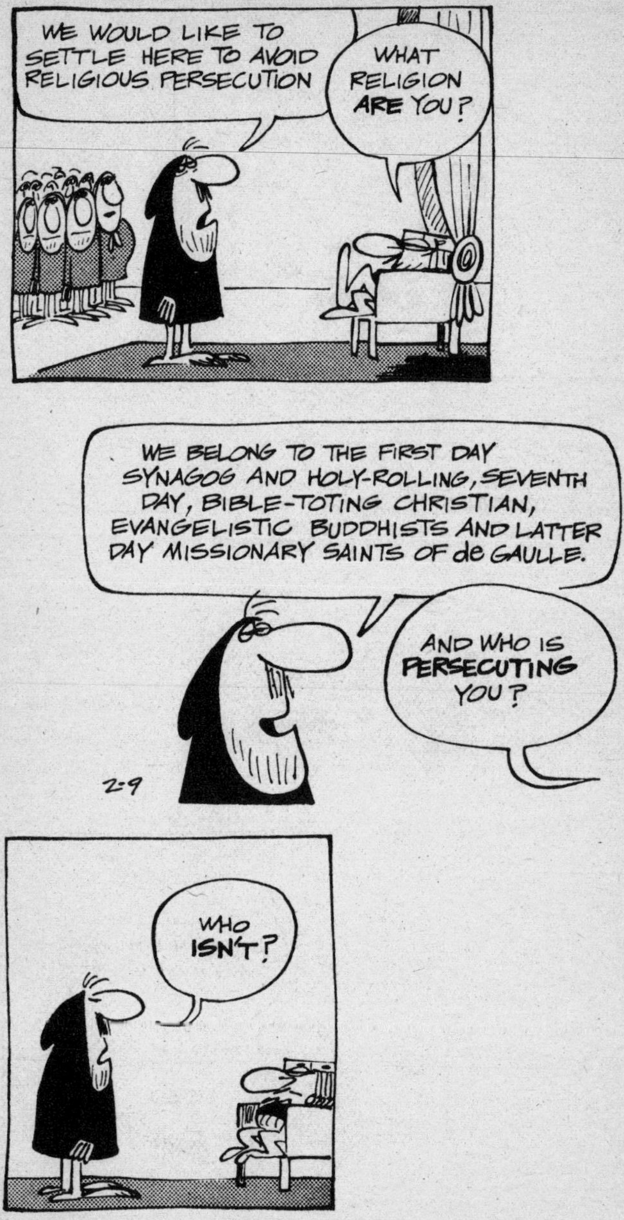
WE WOULD LIKE TO SETTLE HERE TO AVOID RELIGIOUS PERSECUTION
WHAT RELIGION ARE YOU?
WE BELONG TO THE FIRST DAY SYNAGOG AND HOLY-ROLLING, SEVENTH DAY, BIBLE-TOTING CHRISTIAN, EVANGELISTIC BUDDHISTS AND LATTER DAY MISSIONARY SAINTS OF de GAULLE.
AND WHO IS PERSECUTING YOU?
2-9
WHO ISN'T?

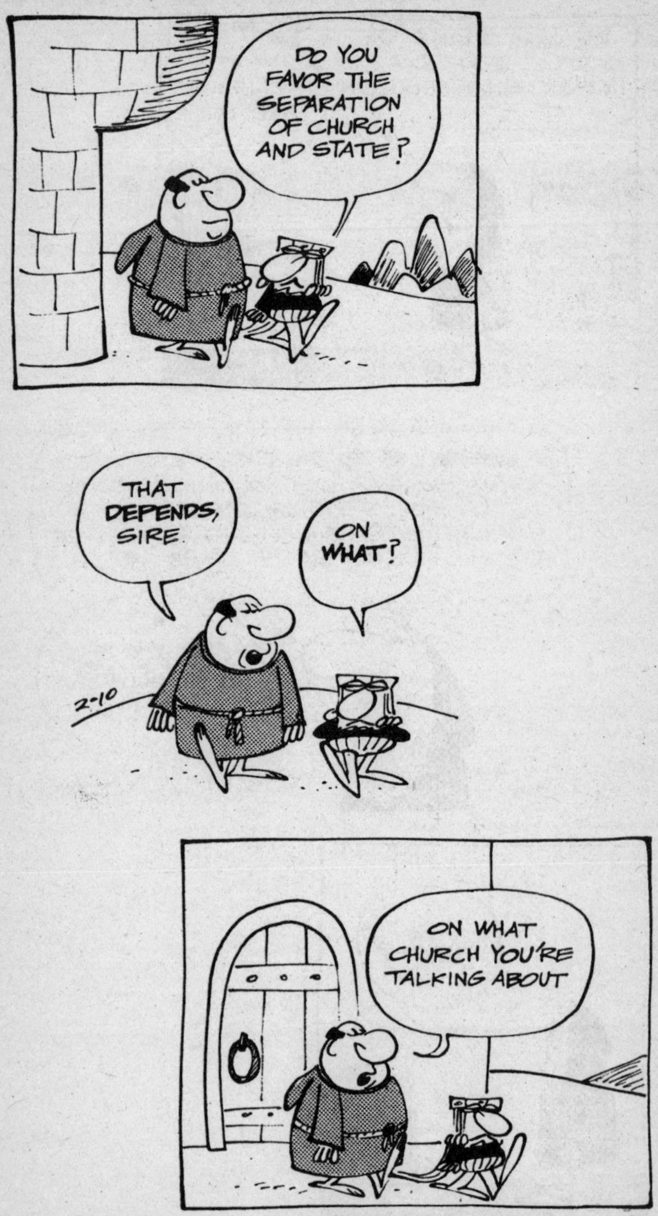
DO YOU FAVOR THE SEPARATION OF CHURCH AND STATE?
THAT DEPENDS, SIRE.
ON WHAT?
2-10
ON WHAT CHURCH YOU'RE TALKING ABOUT

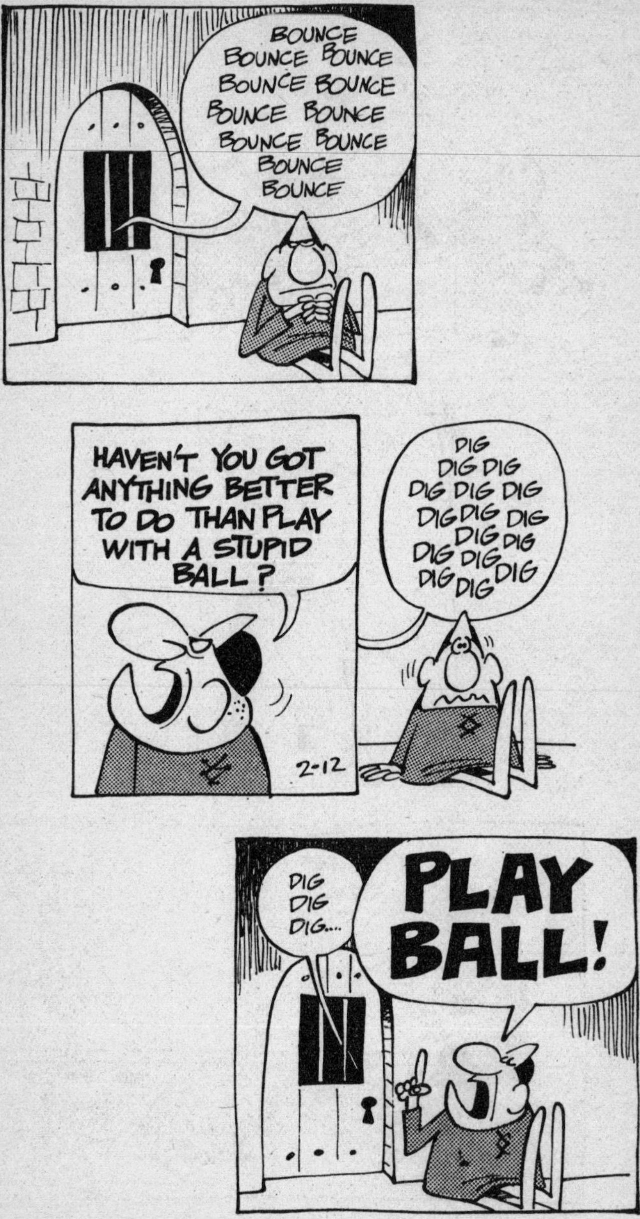
BOUNCE BOUNCE BOUNCE BOUNCE BOUNCE BOUNCE BOUNCE BOUNCE BOUNCE BOUNCE BOUNCE
HAVEN'T YOU GOT ANYTHING BETTER TO DO THAN PLAY WITH A STUPID BALL?
DIG DIG DIG DIG DIG DIG DIG DIG DIG DIG DIG DIG DIG DIG DIG DIG
2-12
DIG DIG DIG....
PLAY BALL!

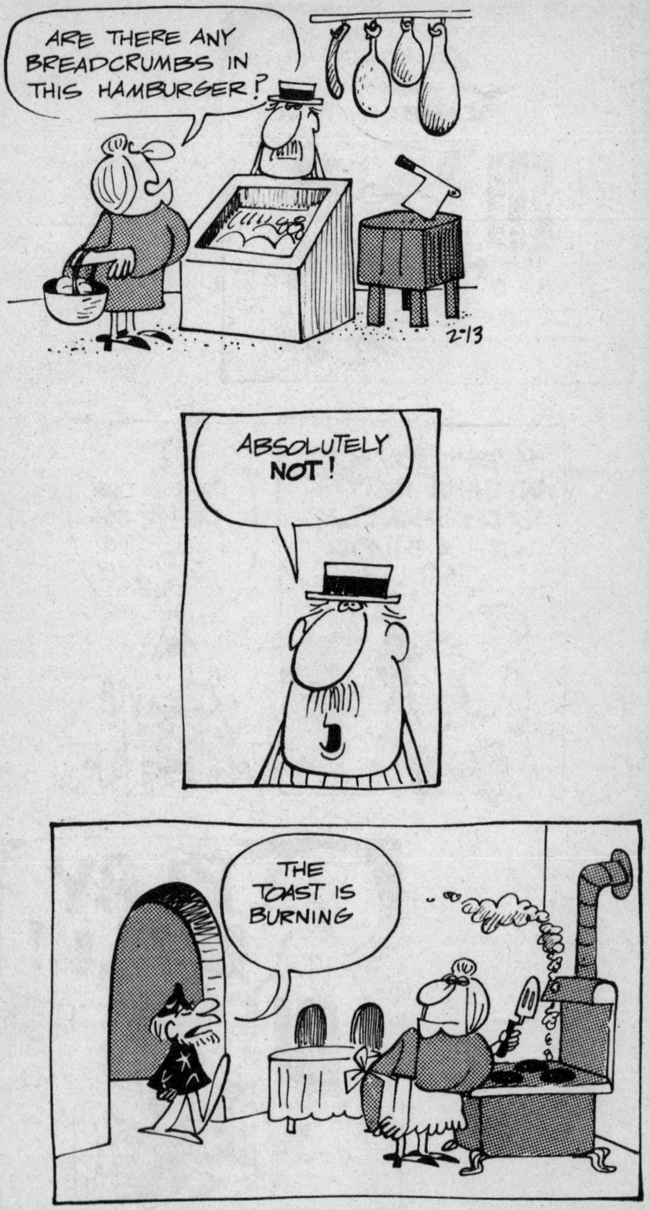
ARE THERE ANY BREADCRUMBS IN THIS HAMBURGER?
2-13
ABSOLUTELY NOT!
THE TOAST IS BURNING

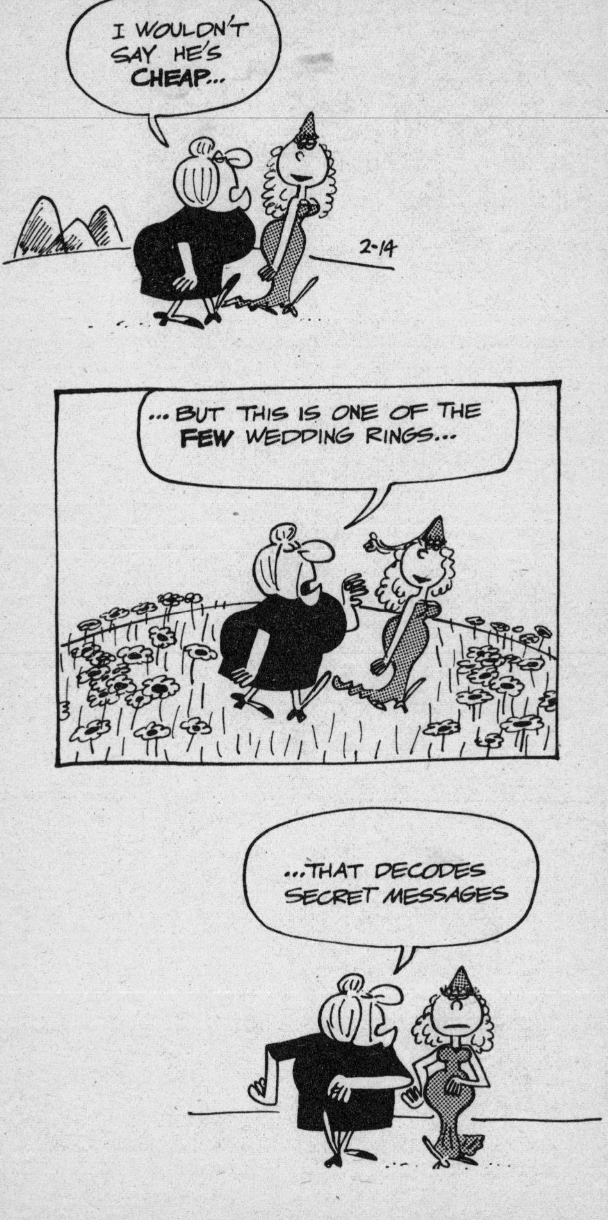
I WOULDN'T SAY HE'S **CHEAP**...
2-14
...BUT THIS IS ONE OF THE **FEW** WEDDING RINGS...
...THAT DECODES SECRET MESSAGES

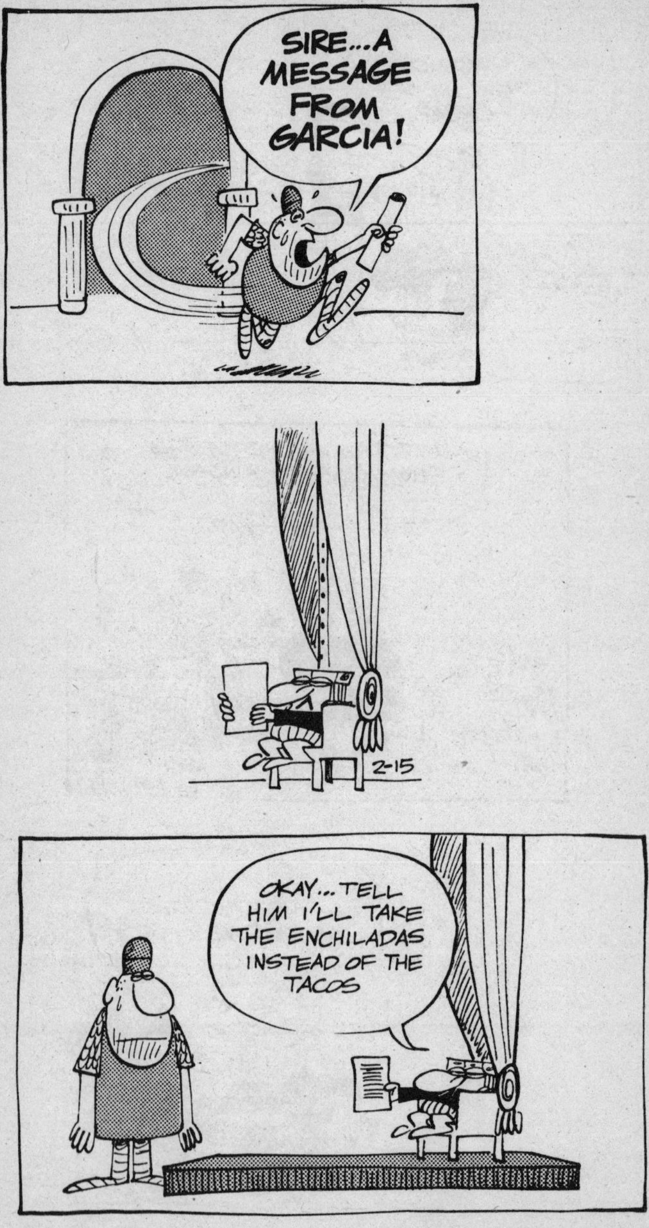
SIRE...A MESSAGE FROM GARCIA!
2-15
OKAY...TELL HIM I'LL TAKE THE ENCHILADAS INSTEAD OF THE TACOS

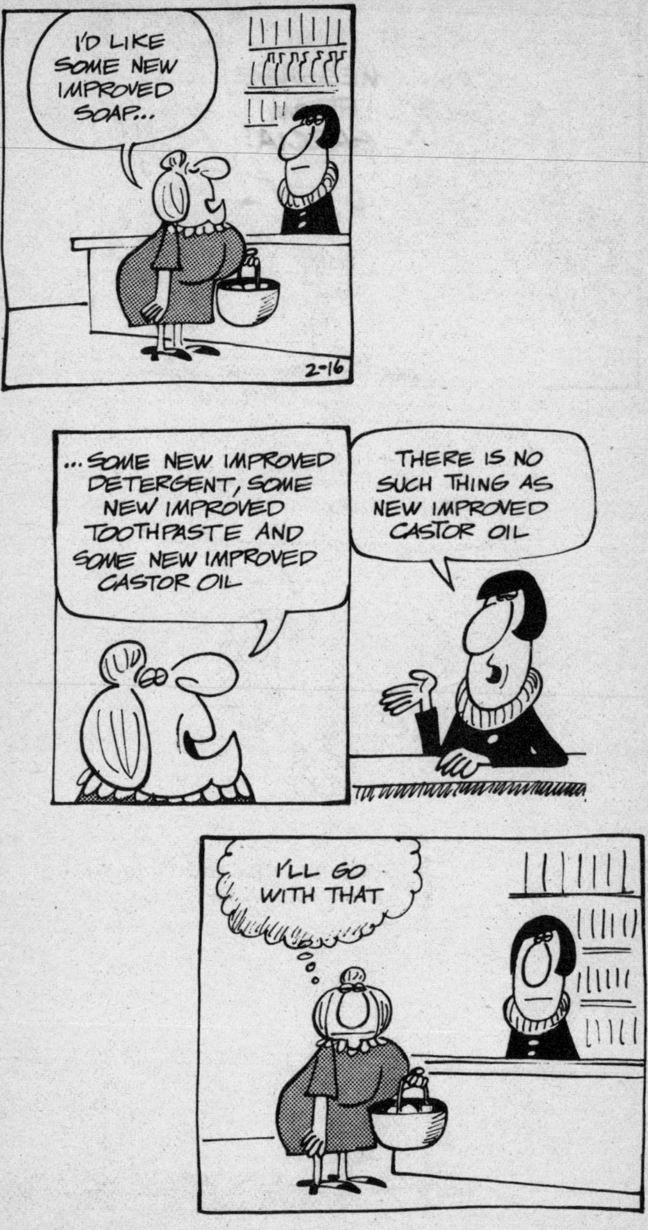
I'D LIKE SOME NEW IMPROVED SOAP...
2-16
...SOME NEW IMPROVED DETERGENT, SOME NEW IMPROVED TOOTHPASTE AND SOME NEW IMPROVED CASTOR OIL
THERE IS NO SUCH THING AS NEW IMPROVED CASTOR OIL
I'LL GO WITH THAT

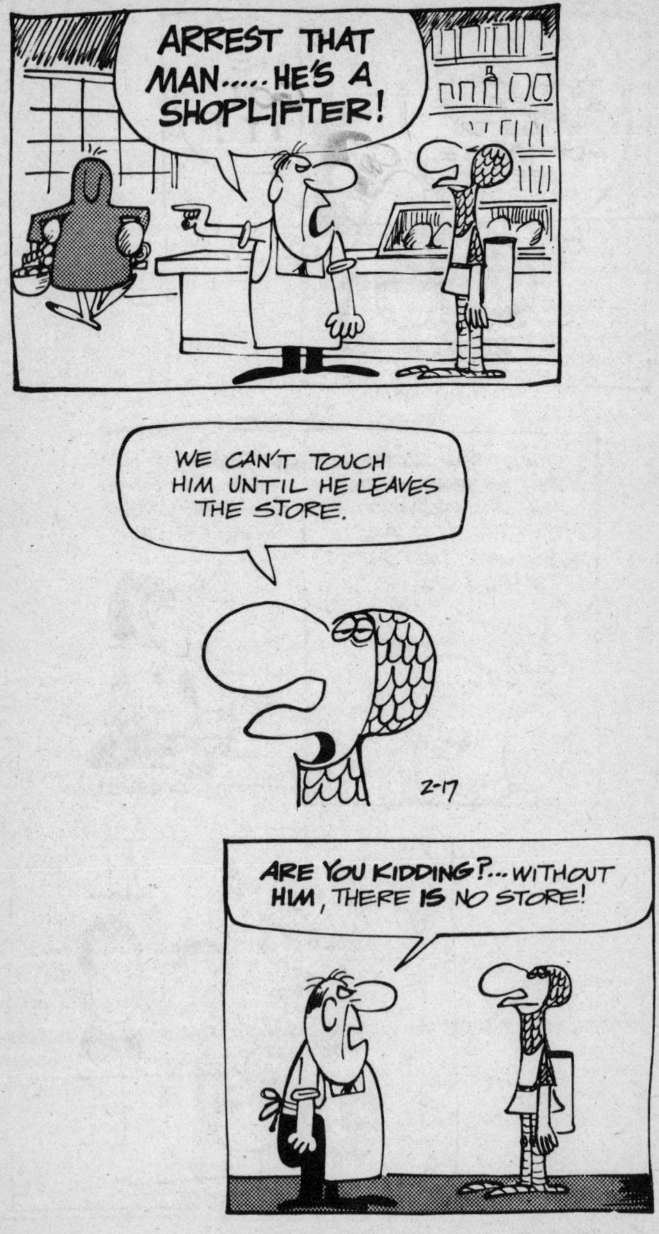
ARREST THAT MAN.....HE'S A SHOPLIFTER!
WE CAN'T TOUCH HIM UNTIL HE LEAVES THE STORE.
2-17
ARE YOU KIDDING?...WITHOUT HIM, THERE IS NO STORE!

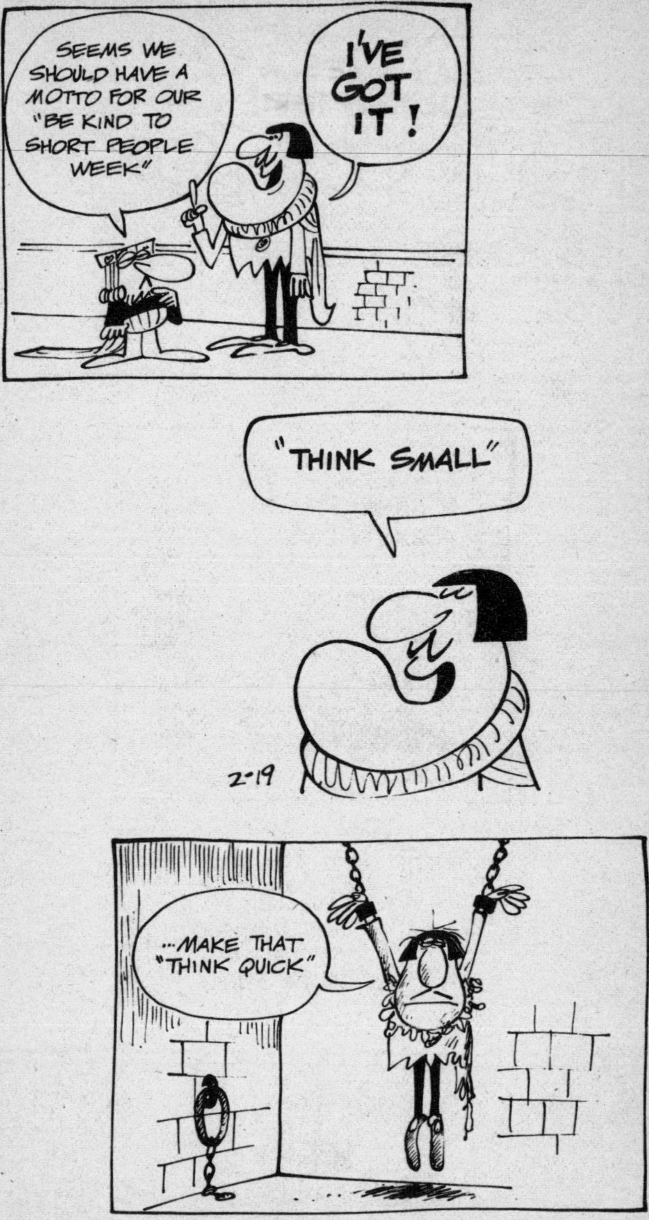
SEEMS WE SHOULD HAVE A MOTTO FOR OUR "BE KIND TO SHORT PEOPLE WEEK"
I'VE GOT IT!
"THINK SMALL"
2-19
...MAKE THAT "THINK QUICK"

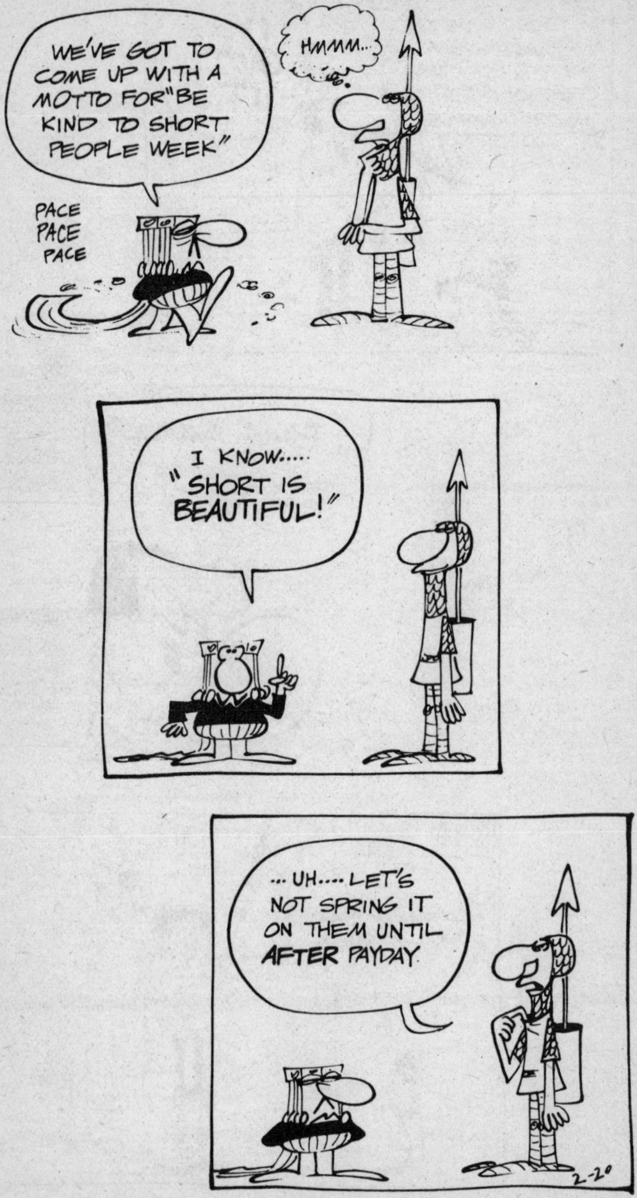
WE'VE GOT TO COME UP WITH A MOTTO FOR "BE KIND TO SHORT PEOPLE WEEK"
HMMM...
PACE PACE PACE
I KNOW..... "SHORT IS BEAUTIFUL!"
...UH.... LET'S NOT SPRING IT ON THEM UNTIL AFTER PAYDAY.
2-20

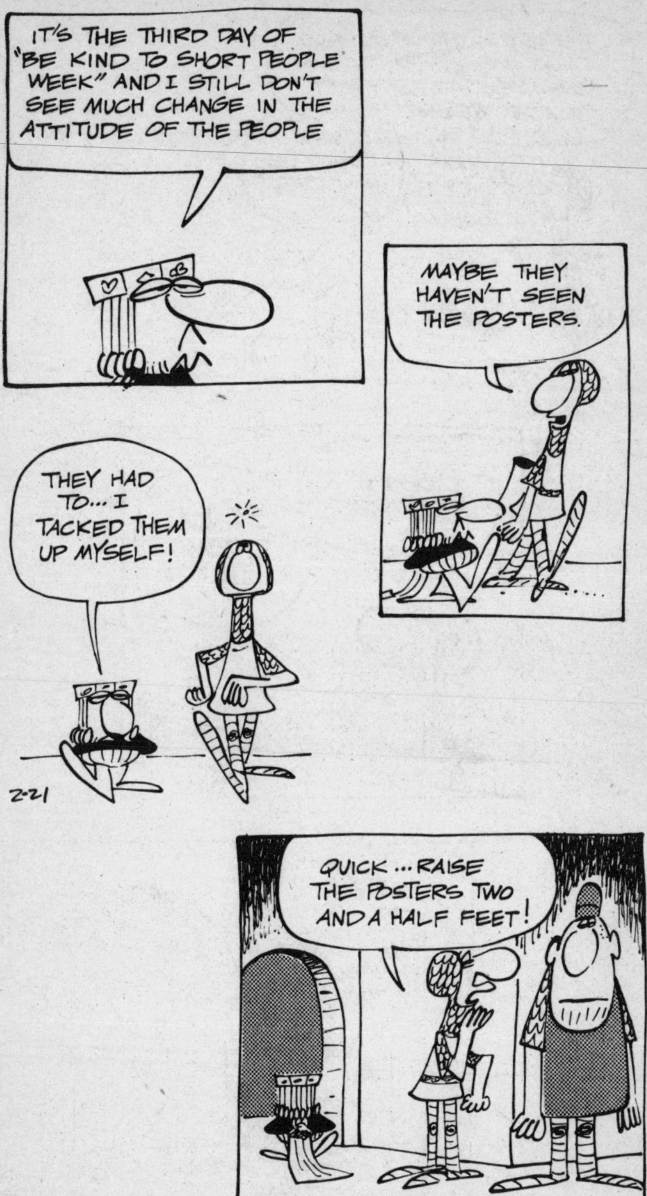
IT'S THE THIRD DAY OF "BE KIND TO SHORT PEOPLE WEEK" AND I STILL DON'T SEE MUCH CHANGE IN THE ATTITUDE OF THE PEOPLE
MAYBE THEY HAVEN'T SEEN THE POSTERS.
THEY HAD TO... I TACKED THEM UP MYSELF!
2-21
QUICK ... RAISE THE POSTERS TWO AND A HALF FEET!

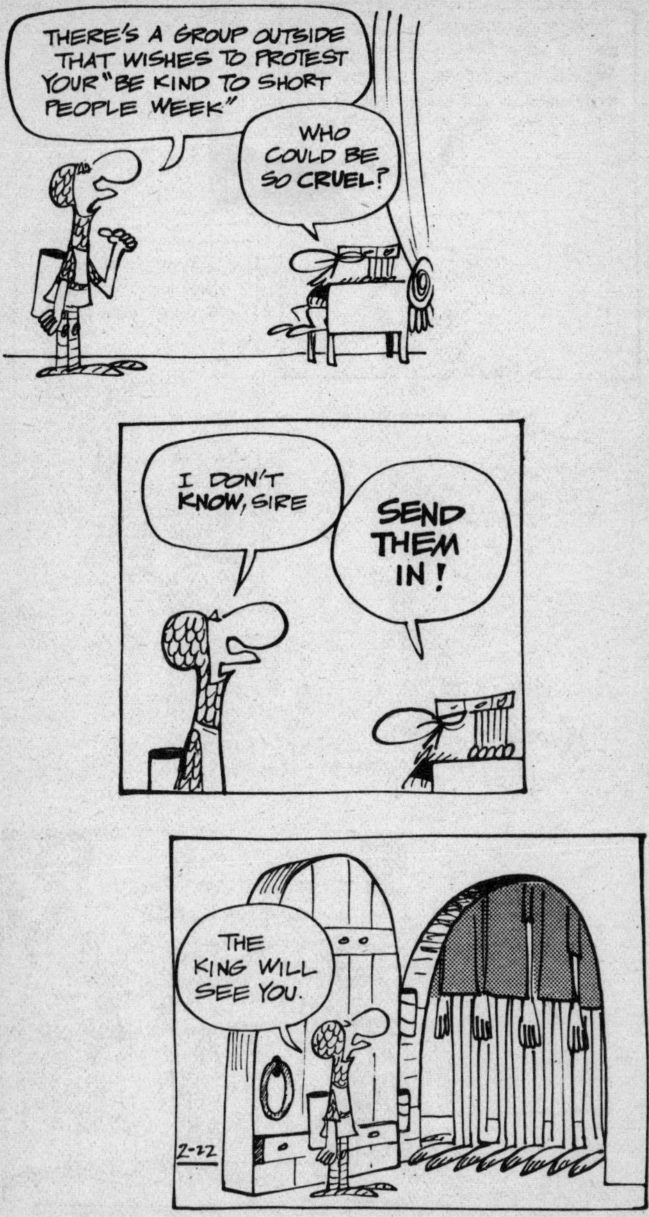
THERE'S A GROUP OUTSIDE THAT WISHES TO PROTEST YOUR "BE KIND TO SHORT PEOPLE WEEK"
WHO COULD BE SO CRUEL?
I DON'T KNOW, SIRE
SEND THEM IN!
THE KING WILL SEE YOU.
2-22

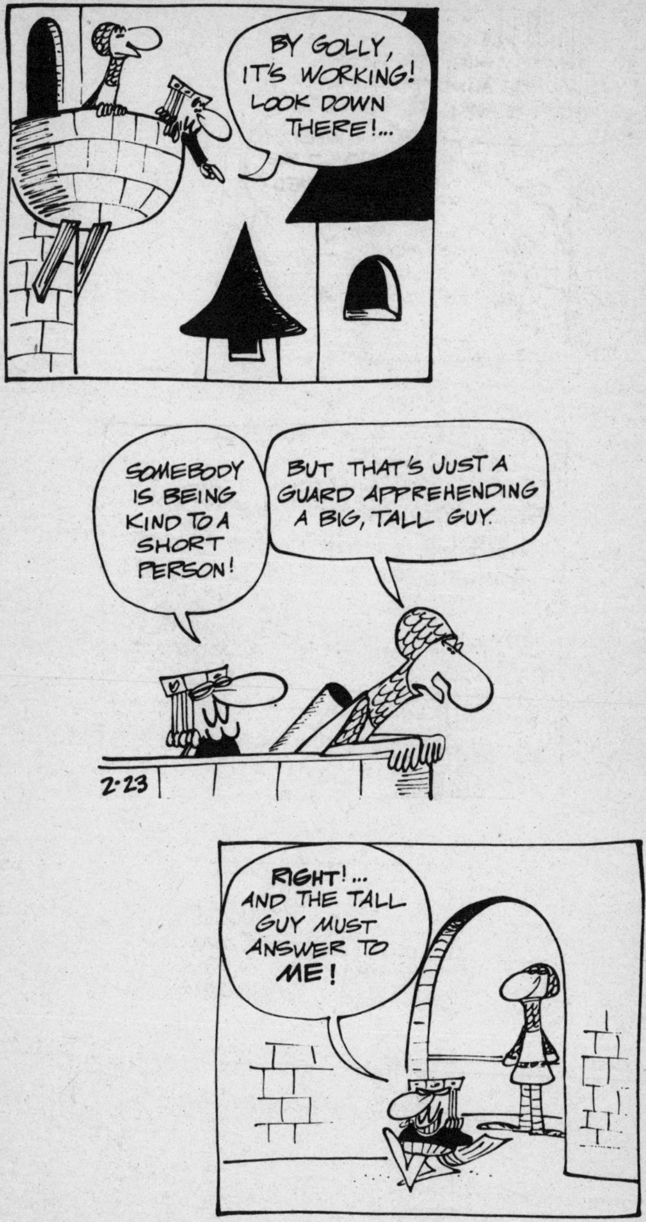
BY GOLLY, IT'S WORKING! LOOK DOWN THERE!...
SOMEBODY IS BEING KIND TO A SHORT PERSON!
BUT THAT'S JUST A GUARD APPREHENDING A BIG, TALL GUY.
2·23
RIGHT!... AND THE TALL GUY MUST ANSWER TO ME!

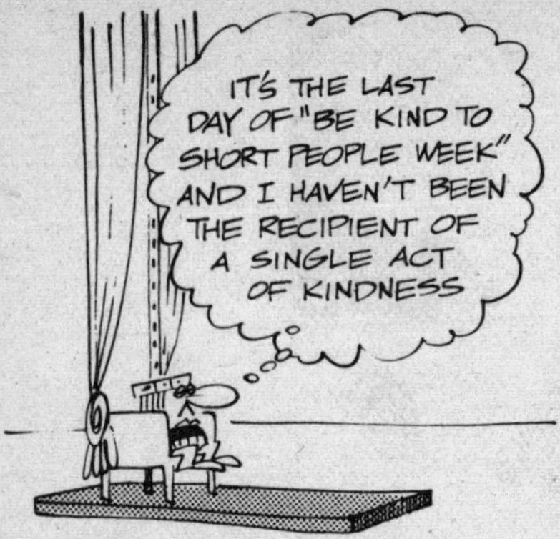
IT'S THE LAST DAY OF "BE KIND TO SHORT PEOPLE WEEK" AND I HAVEN'T BEEN THE RECIPIENT OF A SINGLE ACT OF KINDNESS

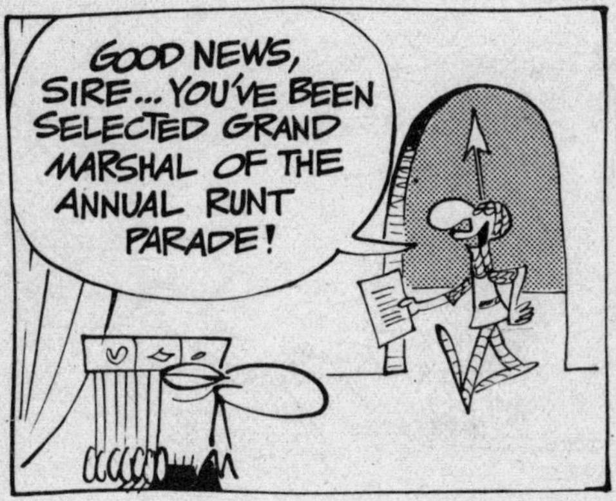
GOOD NEWS, SIRE... YOU'VE BEEN SELECTED GRAND MARSHAL OF THE ANNUAL RUNT PARADE!

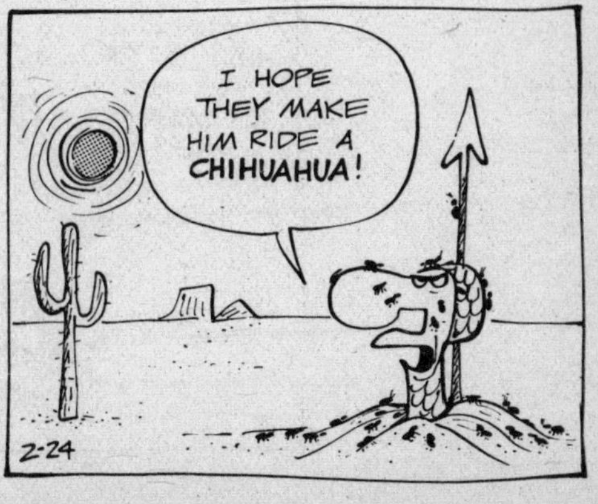
I HOPE THEY MAKE HIM RIDE A CHIHUAHUA!
2-24

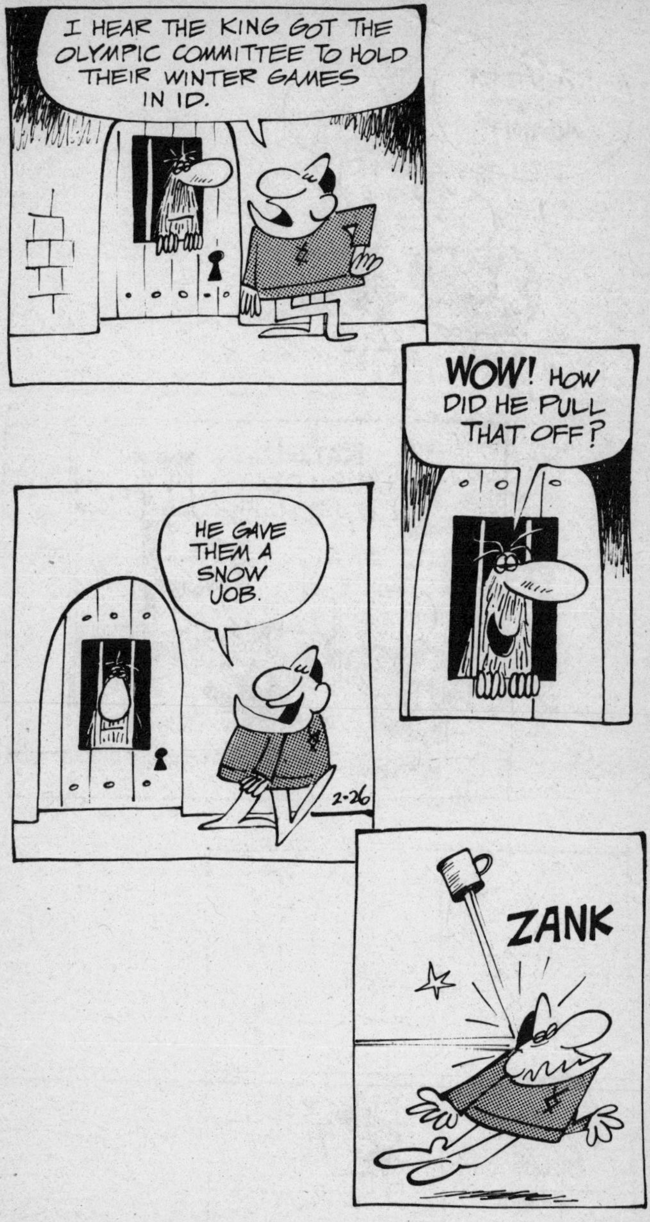
I HEAR THE KING GOT THE OLYMPIC COMMITTEE TO HOLD THEIR WINTER GAMES IN ID.
WOW! HOW DID HE PULL THAT OFF?
HE GAVE THEM A SNOW JOB.
2-26
ZANK

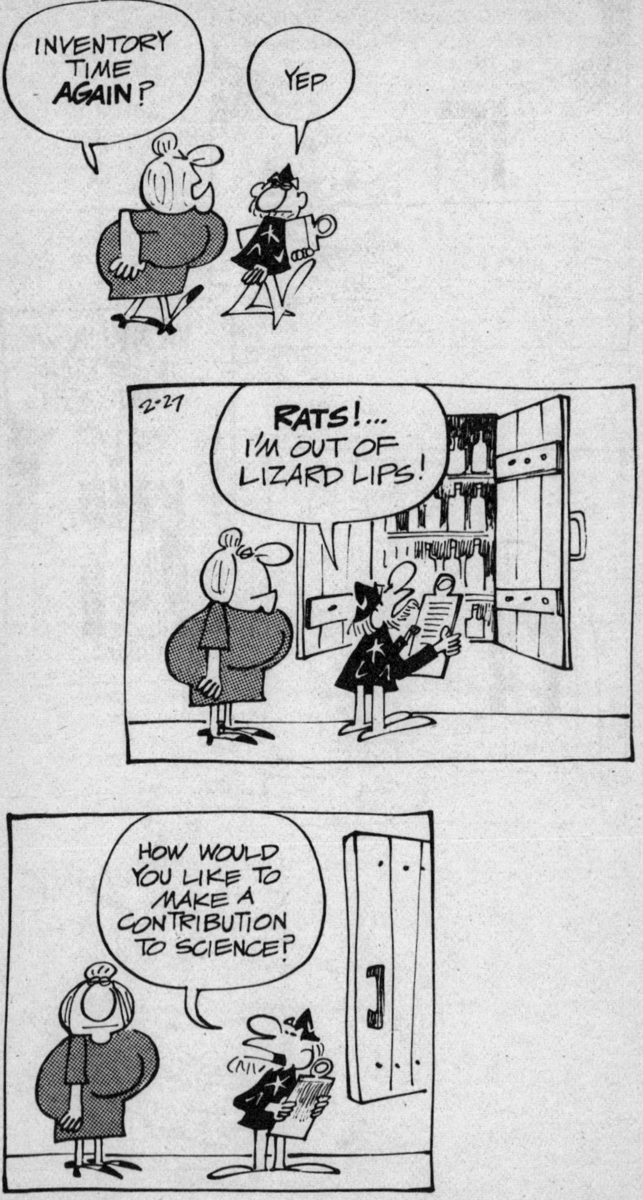
INVENTORY TIME AGAIN?
YEP
2-27
RATS!... I'M OUT OF LIZARD LIPS!
HOW WOULD YOU LIKE TO MAKE A CONTRIBUTION TO SCIENCE?

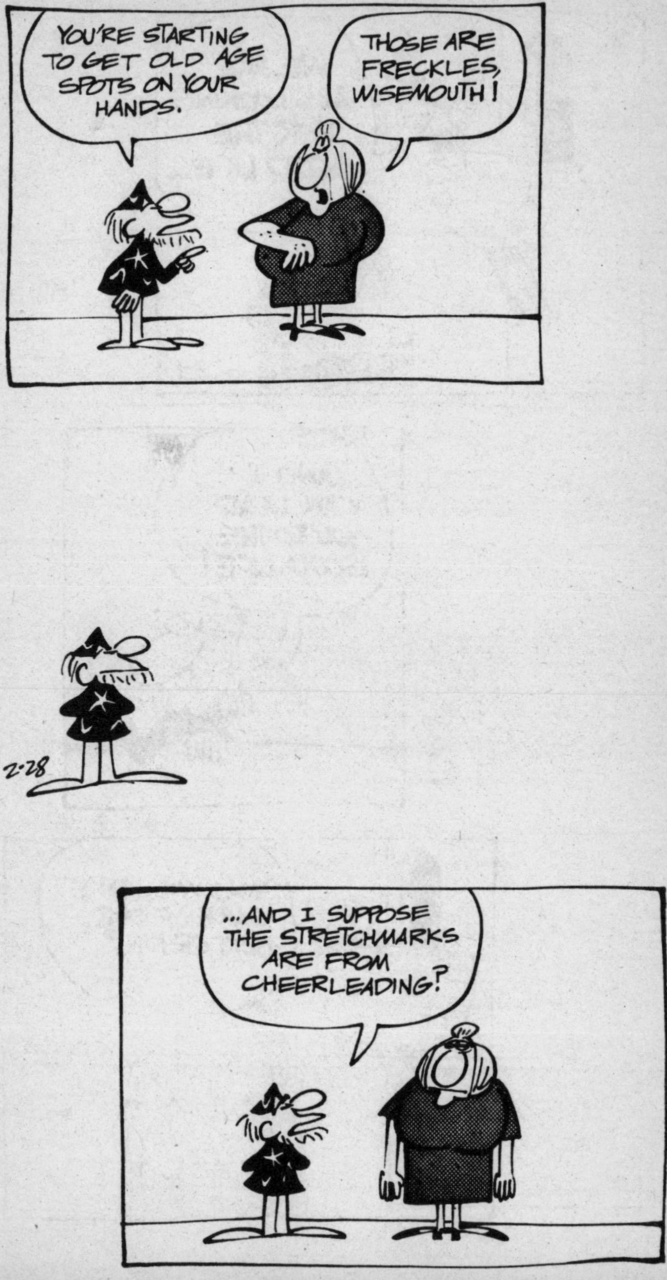
YOU'RE STARTING TO GET OLD AGE SPOTS ON YOUR HANDS.
THOSE ARE FRECKLES, WISEMOUTH!
2·28
...AND I SUPPOSE THE STRETCHMARKS ARE FROM CHEERLEADING?

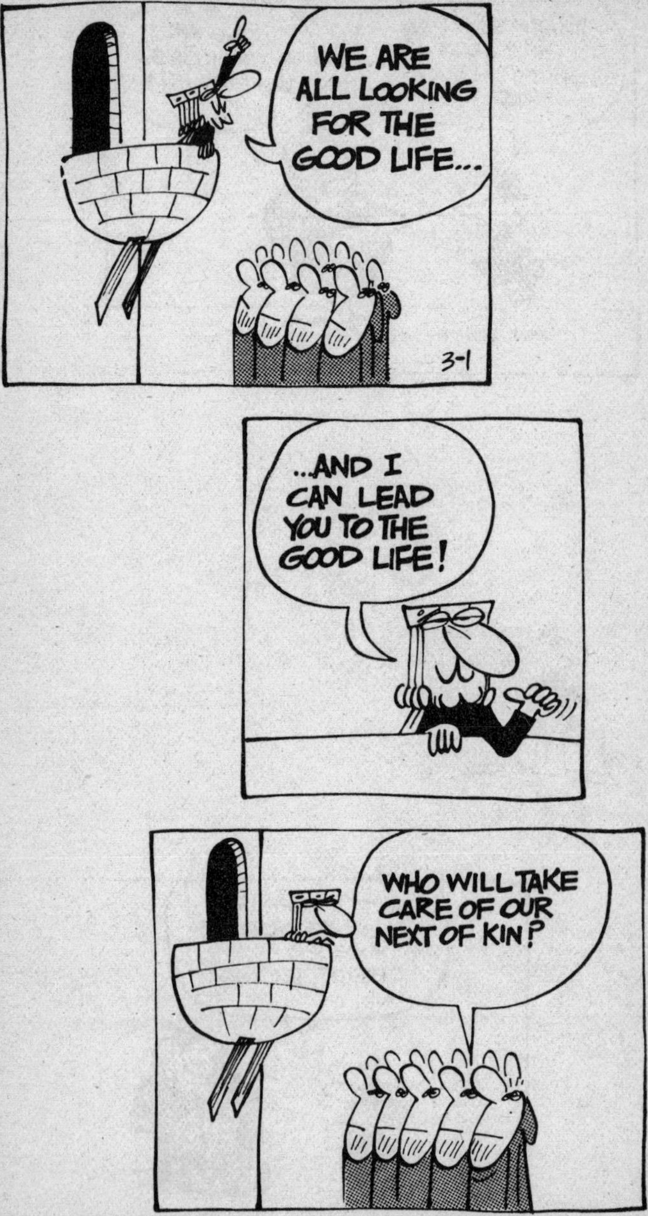
WE ARE ALL LOOKING FOR THE GOOD LIFE...
3-1
...AND I CAN LEAD YOU TO THE GOOD LIFE!
WHO WILL TAKE CARE OF OUR NEXT OF KIN?

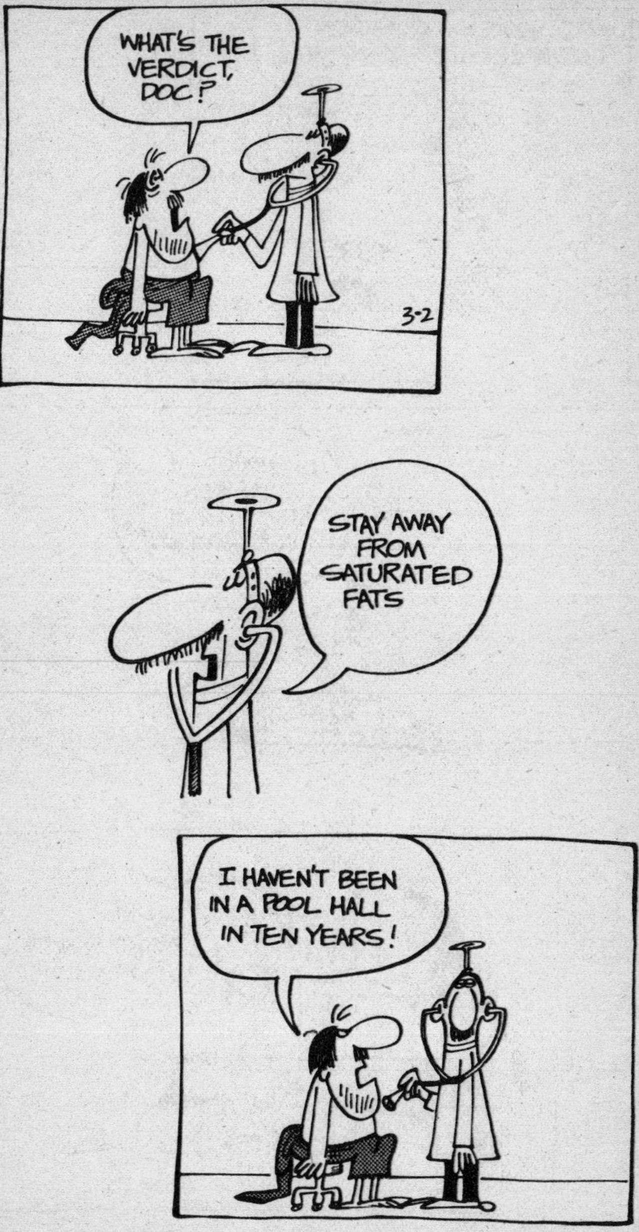
WHAT'S THE VERDICT, DOC?
3-2
STAY AWAY FROM SATURATED FATS
I HAVEN'T BEEN IN A POOL HALL IN TEN YEARS!

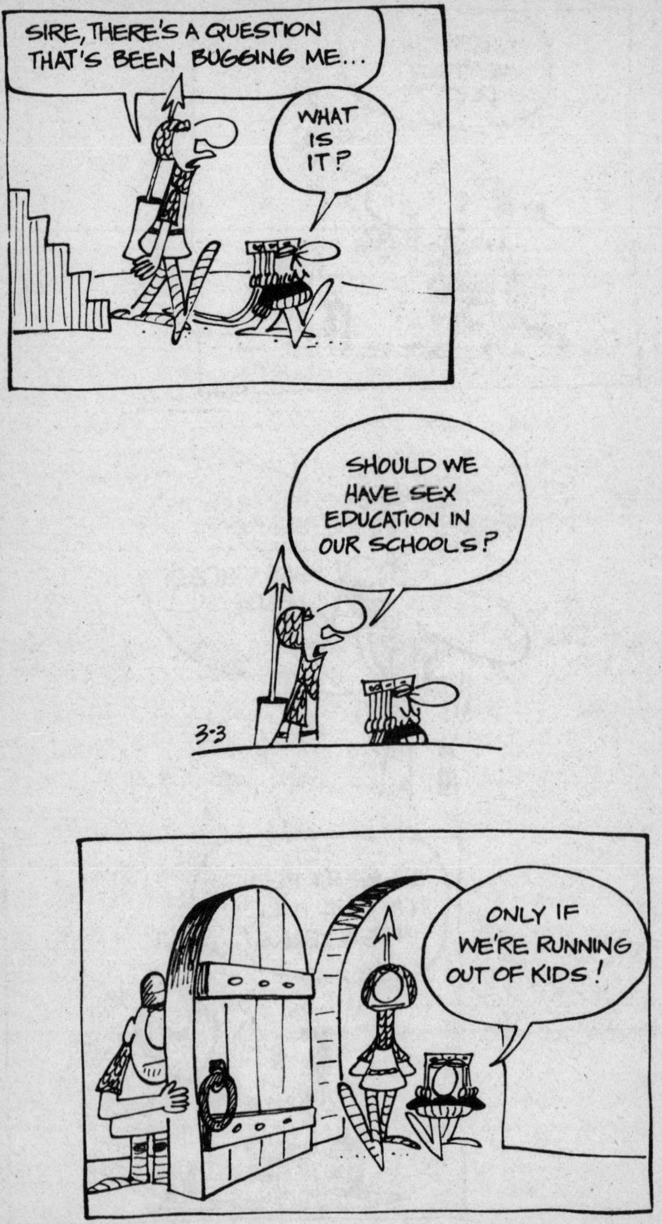
SIRE, THERE'S A QUESTION THAT'S BEEN BUGGING ME...
WHAT IS IT?
SHOULD WE HAVE SEX EDUCATION IN OUR SCHOOLS?
3-3
ONLY IF WE'RE RUNNING OUT OF KIDS!

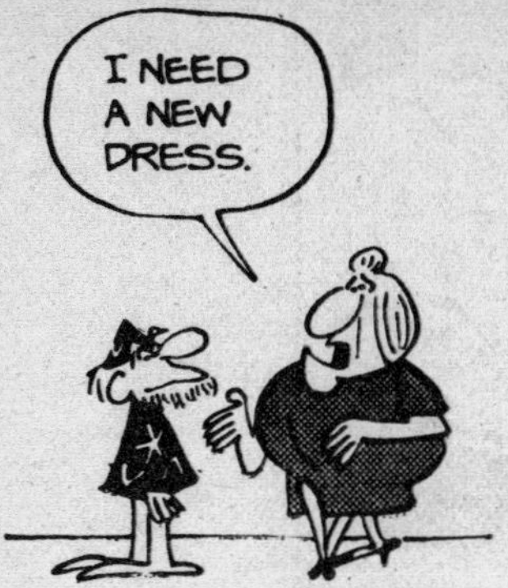
I NEED A NEW DRESS.

95

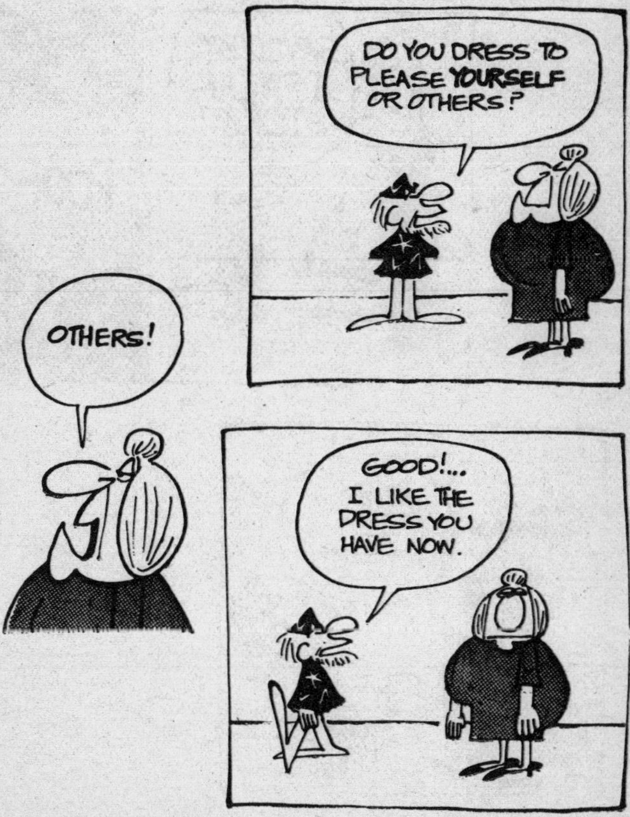
DO YOU DRESS TO PLEASE **YOURSELF** OR OTHERS?
OTHERS!
GOOD!... I LIKE THE DRESS YOU HAVE NOW.

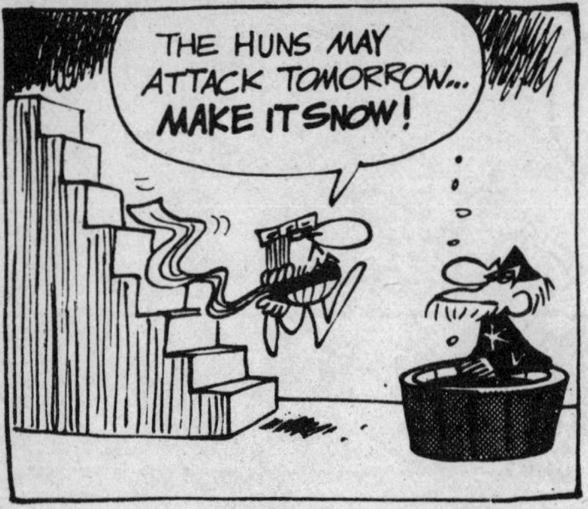
THE HUNS MAY ATTACK TOMORROW... MAKE IT SNOW!

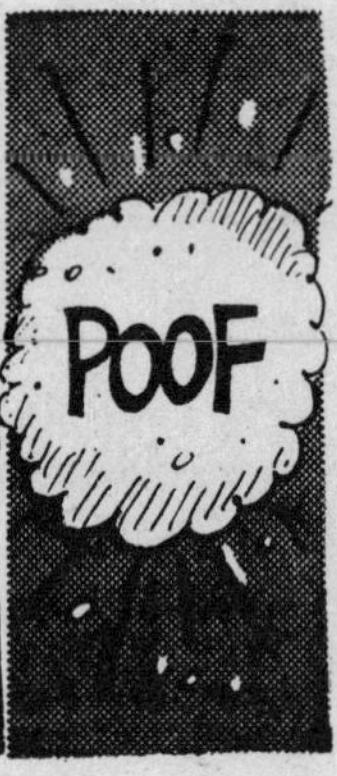
POOF

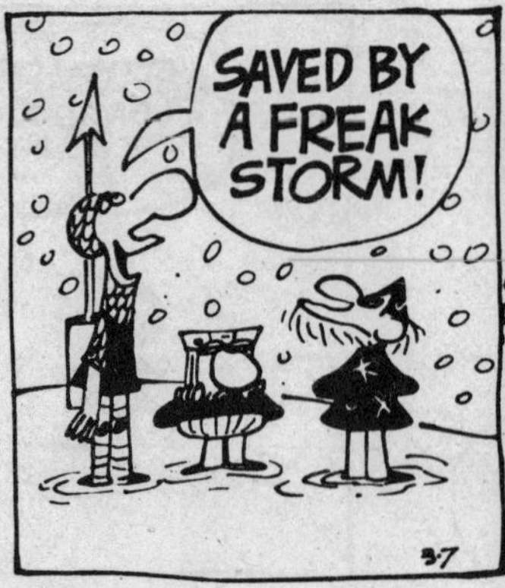
SAVED BY A FREAK STORM!

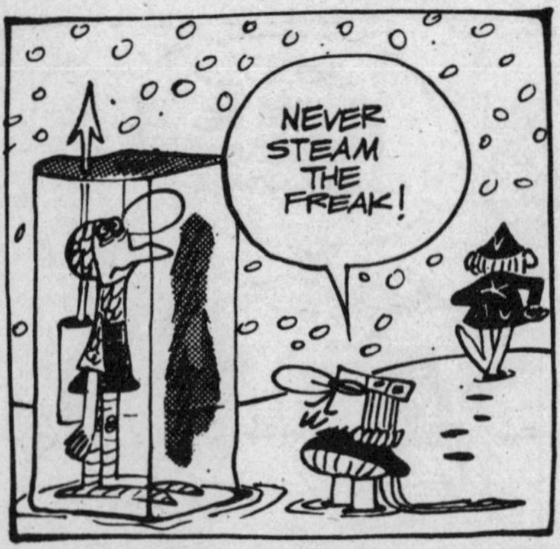
NEVER STEAM THE FREAK!

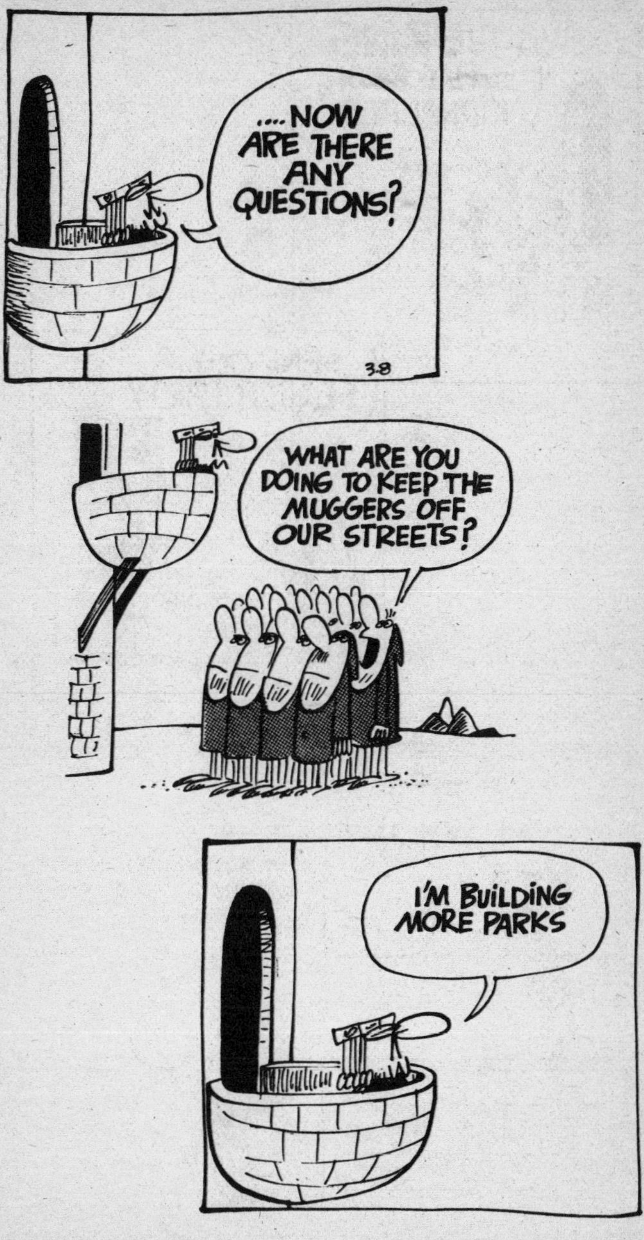
....NOW ARE THERE ANY QUESTIONS?
3-8
WHAT ARE YOU DOING TO KEEP THE MUGGERS OFF OUR STREETS?
I'M BUILDING MORE PARKS

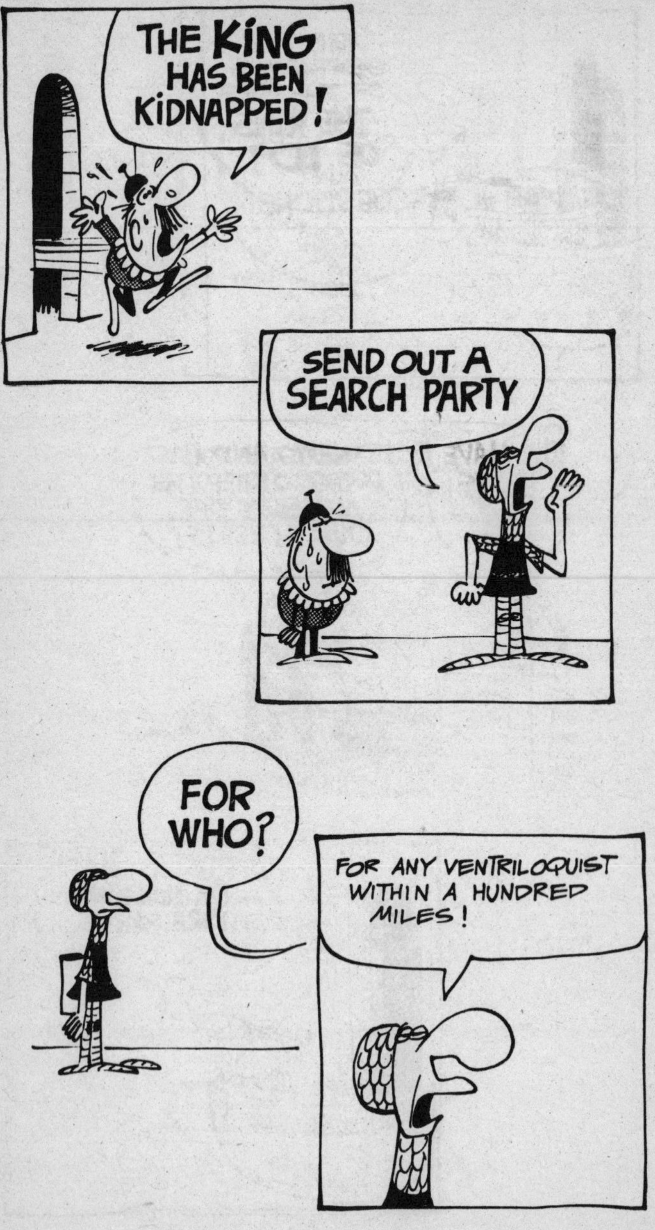
THE KING HAS BEEN KIDNAPPED!
SEND OUT A SEARCH PARTY
FOR WHO?
FOR ANY VENTRILOQUIST WITHIN A HUNDRED MILES!

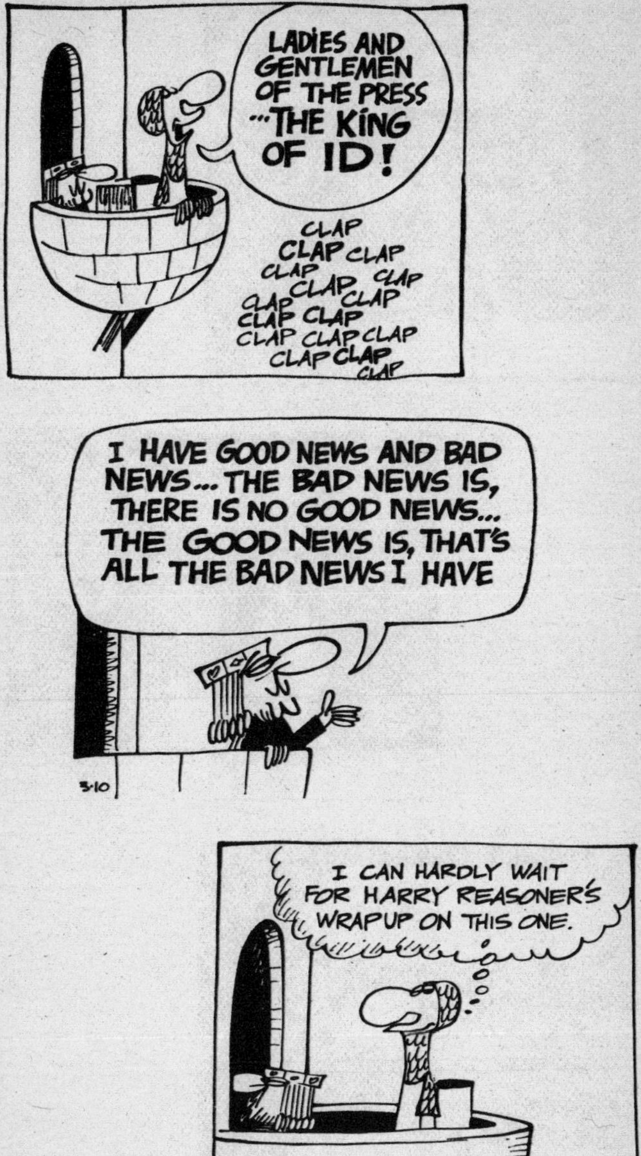
LADIES AND GENTLEMEN OF THE PRESS ...THE KING OF ID!
CLAP
CLAP CLAP
CLAP
CLAP CLAP
CLAP CLAP
CLAP CLAP
CLAP CLAP CLAP
CLAP CLAP
CLAP
I HAVE GOOD NEWS AND BAD NEWS... THE BAD NEWS IS, THERE IS NO GOOD NEWS... THE GOOD NEWS IS, THAT'S ALL THE BAD NEWS I HAVE
3-10
I CAN HARDLY WAIT FOR HARRY REASONER'S WRAPUP ON THIS ONE.

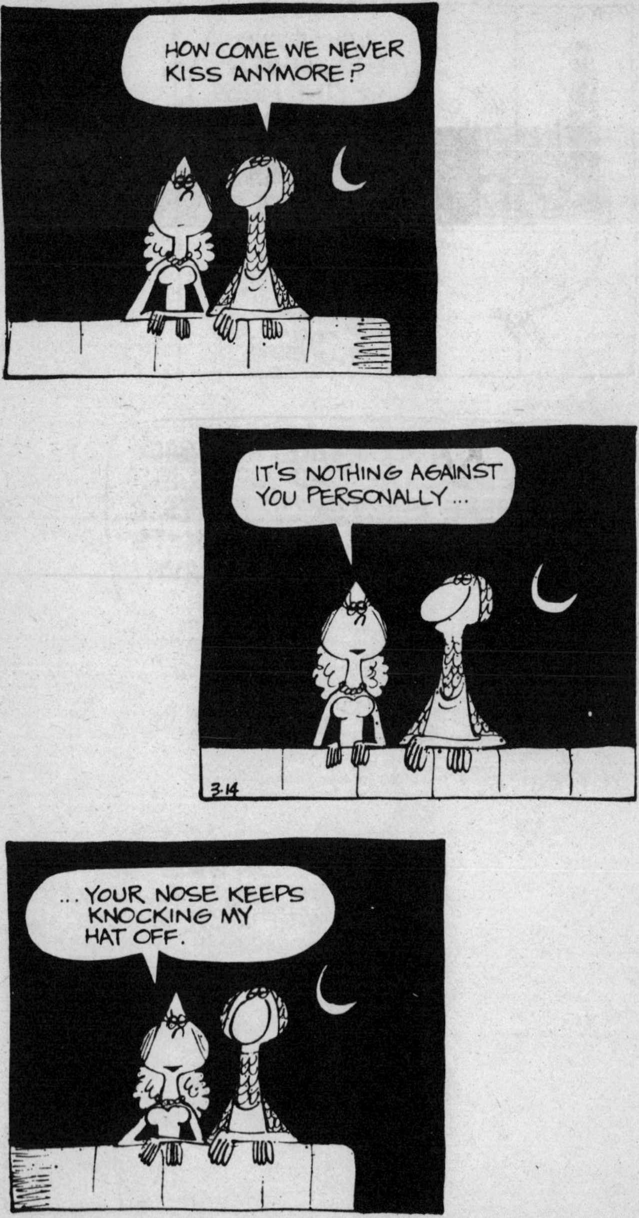
HOW COME WE NEVER KISS ANYMORE?
IT'S NOTHING AGAINST YOU PERSONALLY...
3.14
...YOUR NOSE KEEPS KNOCKING MY HAT OFF.

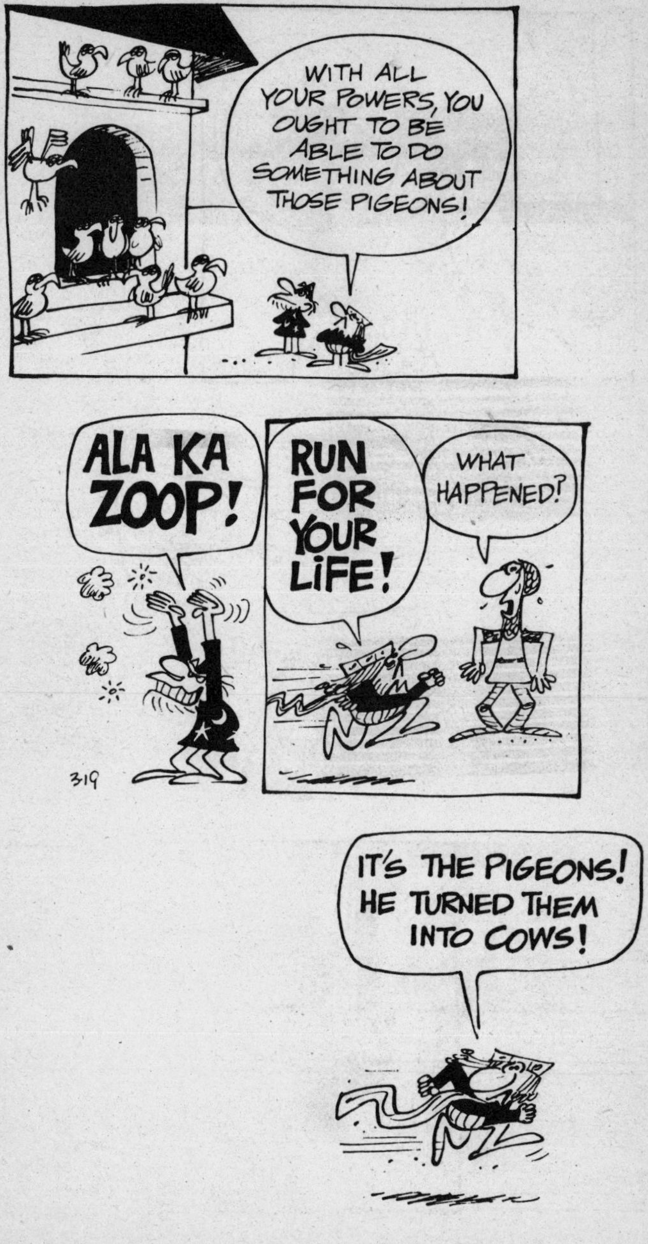
WITH ALL YOUR POWERS, YOU OUGHT TO BE ABLE TO DO SOMETHING ABOUT THOSE PIGEONS!
ALA KA ZOOP!
RUN FOR YOUR LIFE!
WHAT HAPPENED?
IT'S THE PIGEONS! HE TURNED THEM INTO COWS!

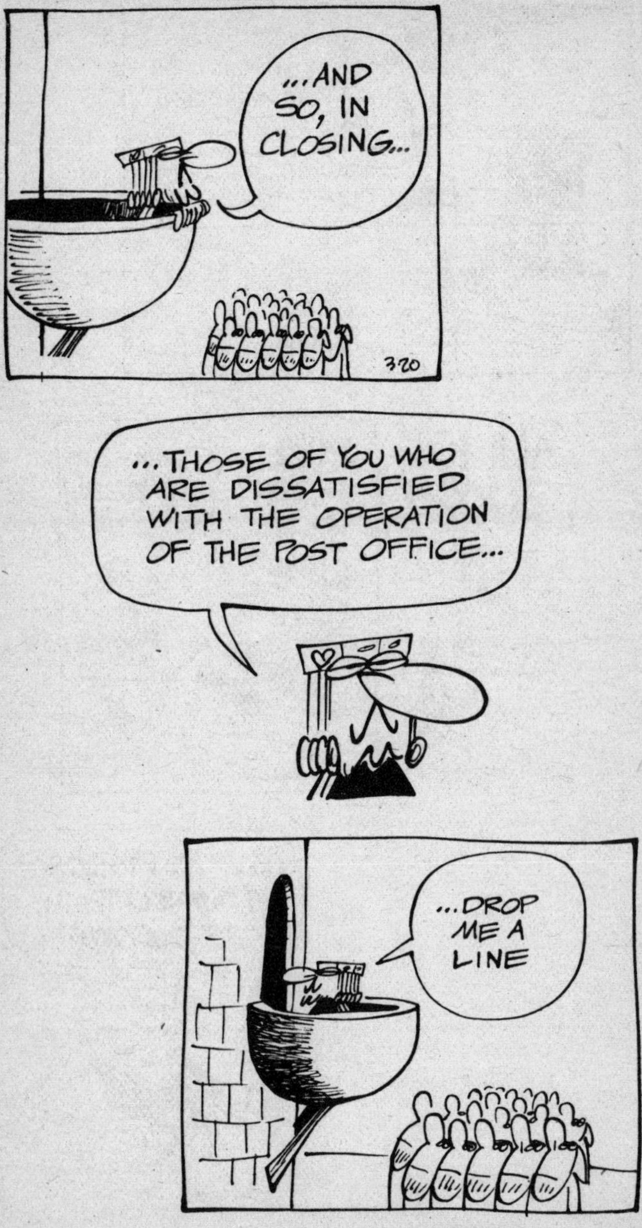
...AND SO, IN CLOSING...
3-20
...THOSE OF YOU WHO ARE DISSATISFIED WITH THE OPERATION OF THE POST OFFICE...
...DROP ME A LINE

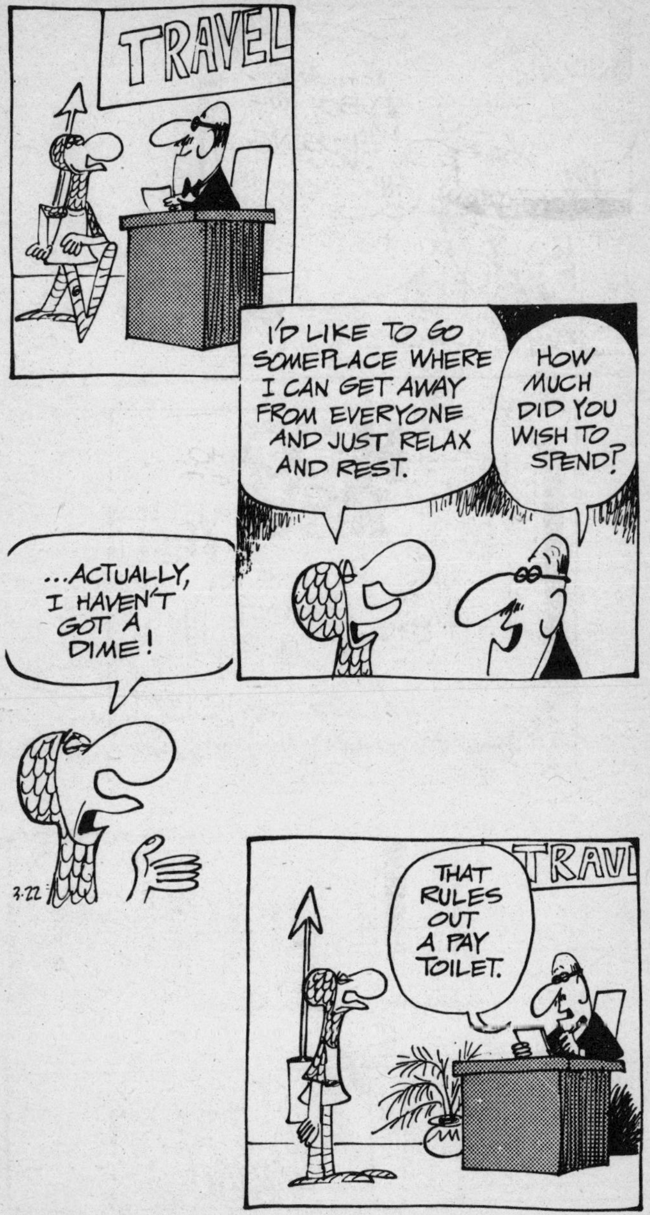
TRAVEL
I'D LIKE TO GO SOMEPLACE WHERE I CAN GET AWAY FROM EVERYONE AND JUST RELAX AND REST.
HOW MUCH DID YOU WISH TO SPEND?
...ACTUALLY, I HAVEN'T GOT A DIME!
3-22
TRAVL
THAT RULES OUT A PAY TOILET.

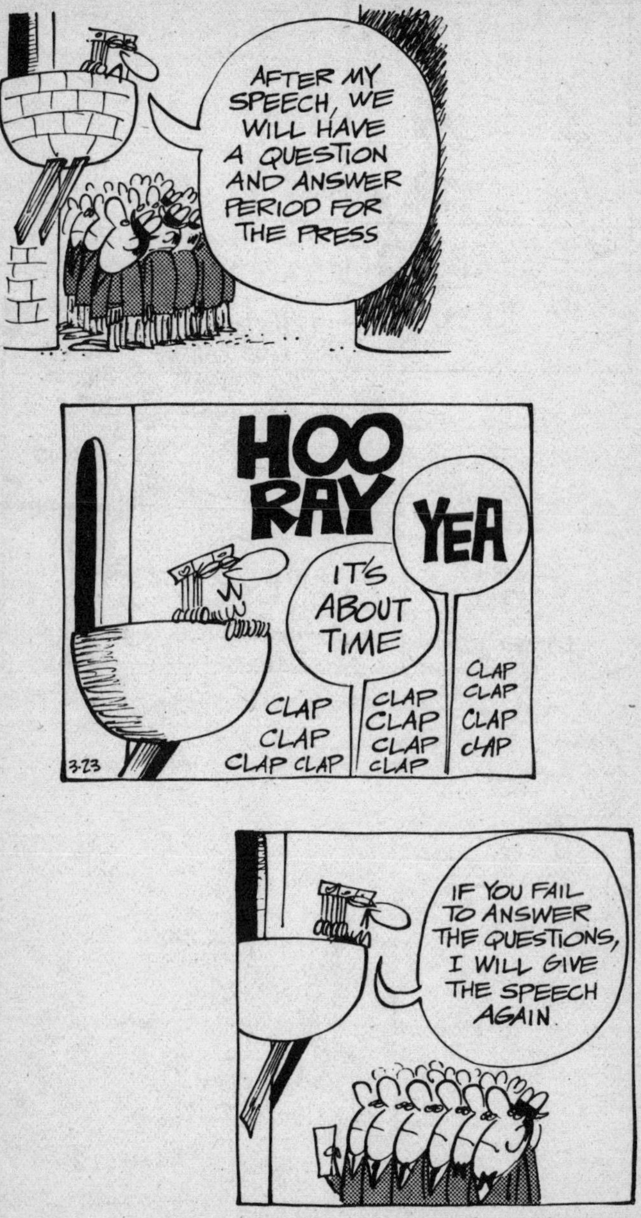
AFTER MY SPEECH, WE WILL HAVE A QUESTION AND ANSWER PERIOD FOR THE PRESS
HOORAY
YEA
IT'S ABOUT TIME
CLAP CLAP CLAP CLAP
CLAP CLAP CLAP CLAP
CLAP CLAP CLAP CLAP
3-23
IF YOU FAIL TO ANSWER THE QUESTIONS, I WILL GIVE THE SPEECH AGAIN.

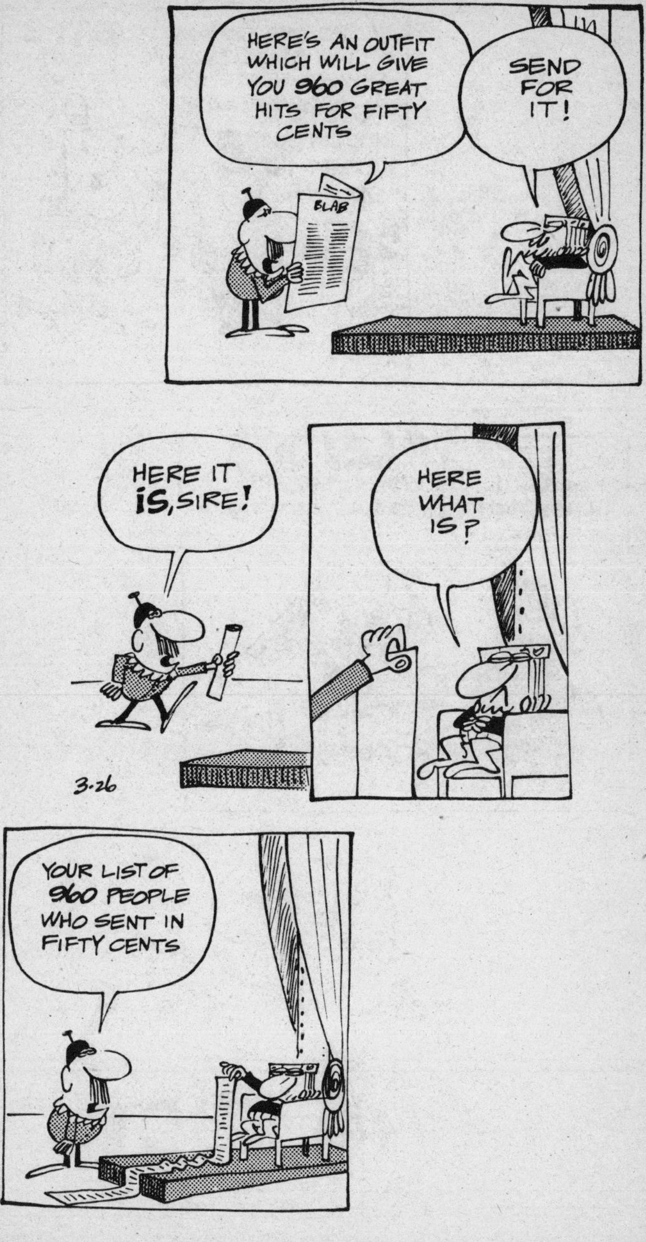

HERE'S AN OUTFIT WHICH WILL GIVE YOU 960 GREAT HITS FOR FIFTY CENTS
SEND FOR IT!
BLAB
HERE IT IS, SIRE!
HERE WHAT IS?
3·26
YOUR LIST OF 960 PEOPLE WHO SENT IN FIFTY CENTS

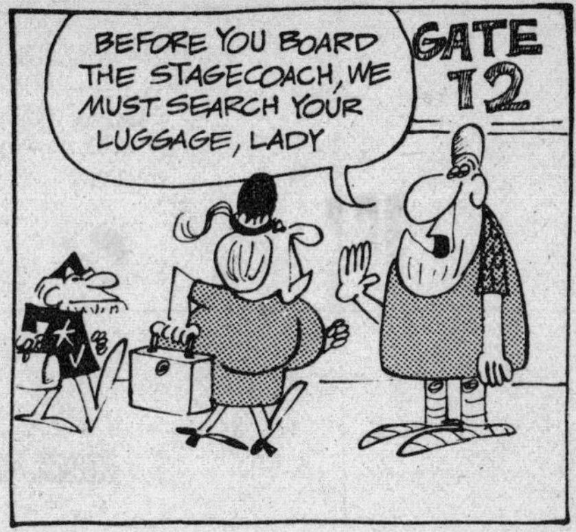
BEFORE YOU BOARD THE STAGECOACH, WE MUST SEARCH YOUR LUGGAGE, LADY
GATE 12

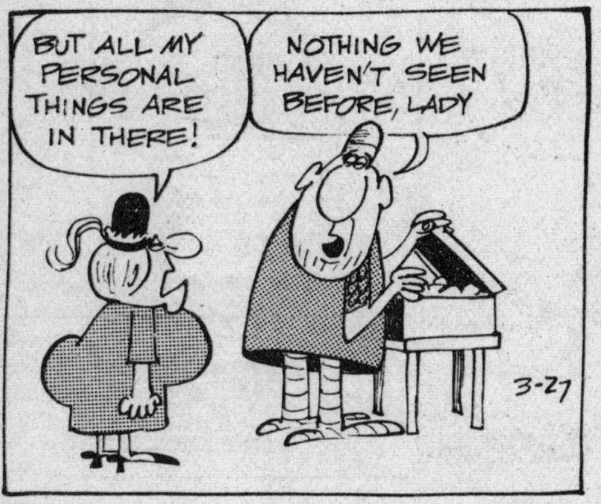
BUT ALL MY PERSONAL THINGS ARE IN THERE!
NOTHING WE HAVEN'T SEEN BEFORE, LADY
3-27

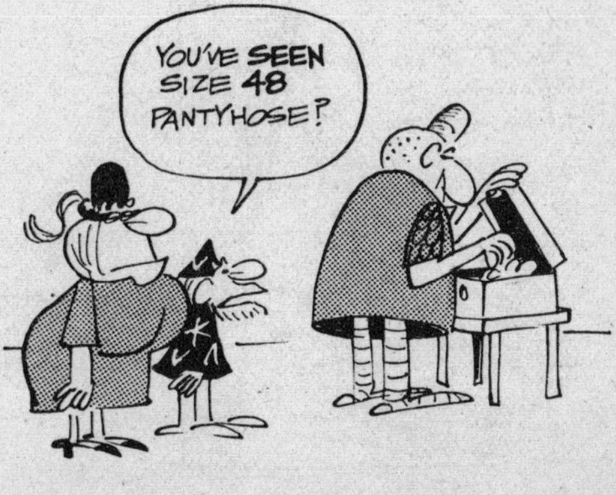
YOU'VE SEEN SIZE 48 PANTYHOSE?

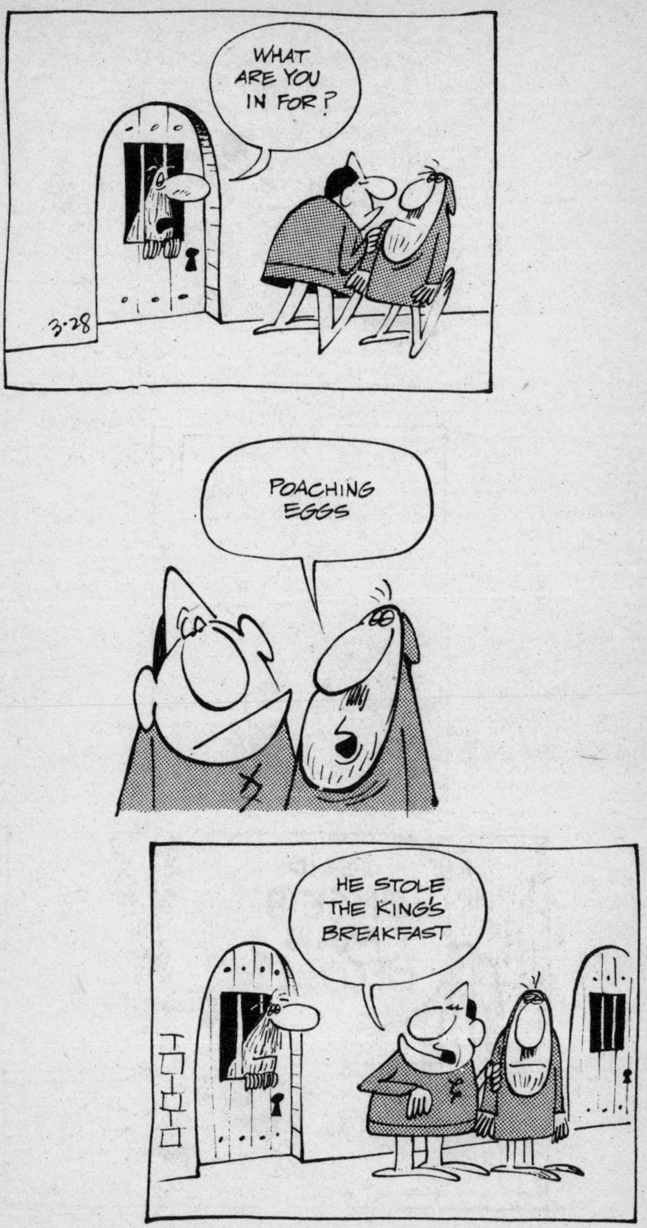
WHAT ARE YOU IN FOR?
3·28
POACHING EGGS
HE STOLE THE KING'S BREAKFAST

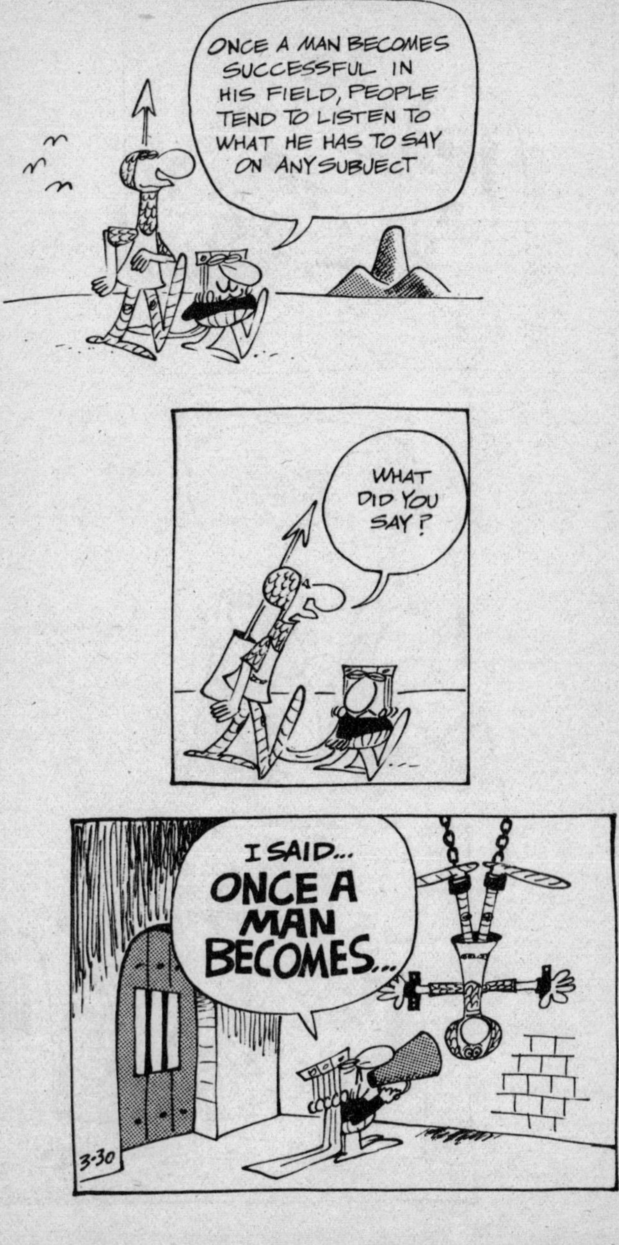
ONCE A MAN BECOMES SUCCESSFUL IN HIS FIELD, PEOPLE TEND TO LISTEN TO WHAT HE HAS TO SAY ON ANY SUBJECT
WHAT DID YOU SAY ?
I SAID... ONCE A MAN BECOMES...
3-30

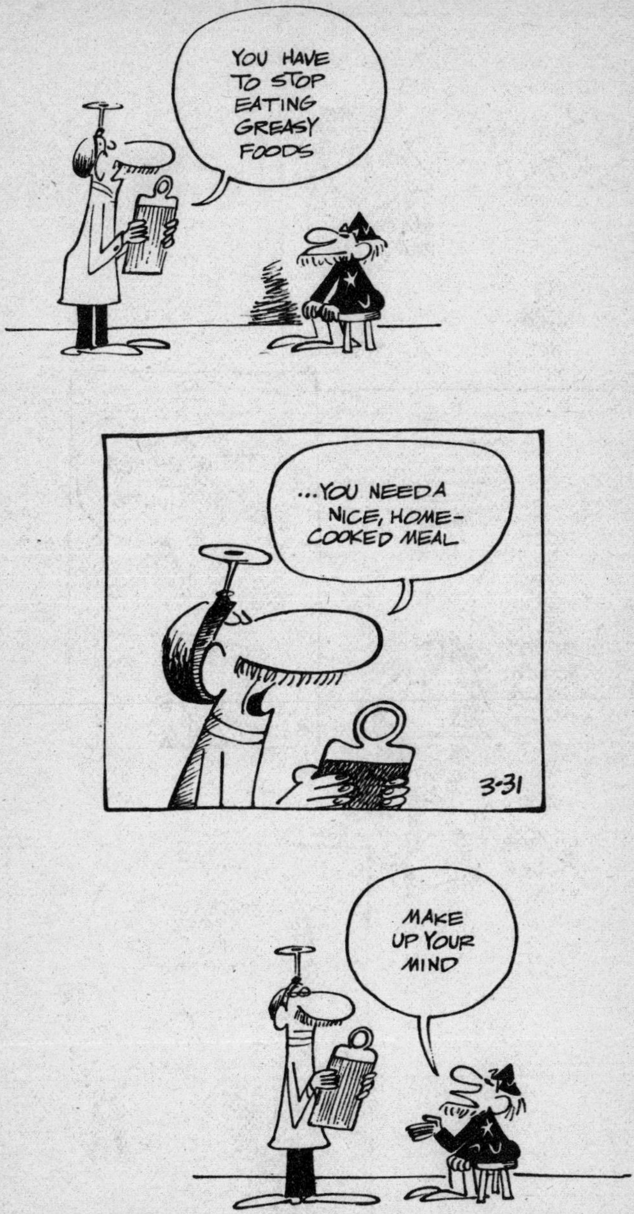
YOU HAVE TO STOP EATING GREASY FOODS
...YOU NEED A NICE, HOME-COOKED MEAL
3-31
MAKE UP YOUR MIND

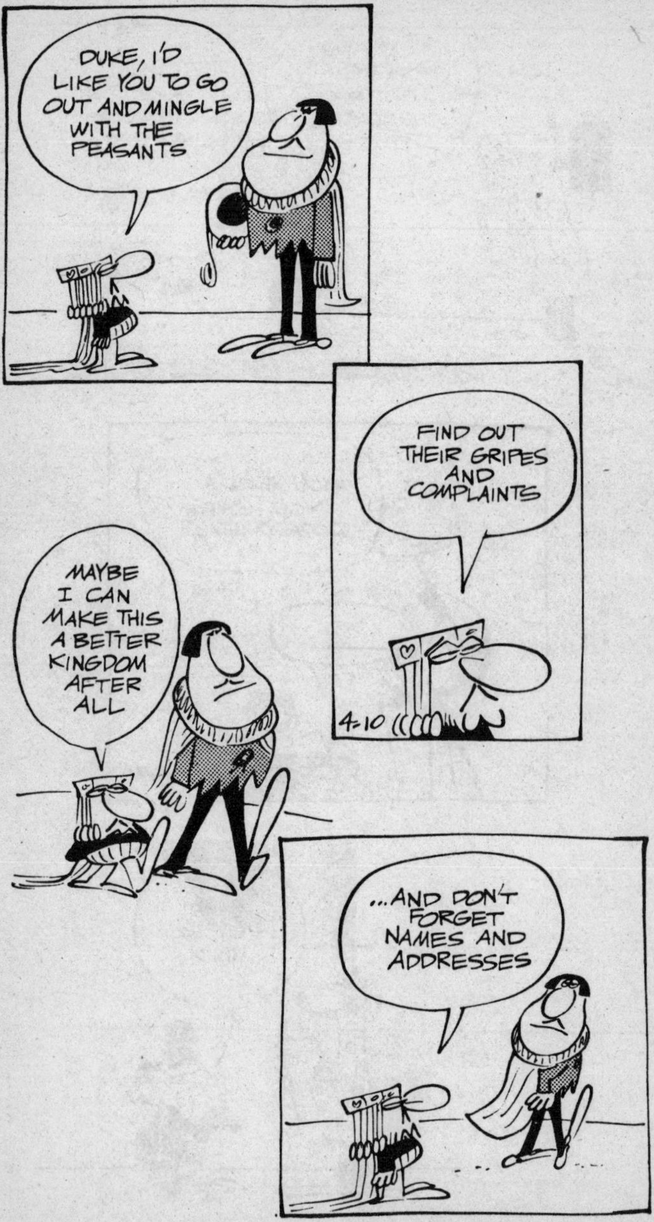
DUKE, I'D LIKE YOU TO GO OUT AND MINGLE WITH THE PEASANTS
FIND OUT THEIR GRIPES AND COMPLAINTS
4-10
MAYBE I CAN MAKE THIS A BETTER KINGDOM AFTER ALL
...AND DON'T FORGET NAMES AND ADDRESSES

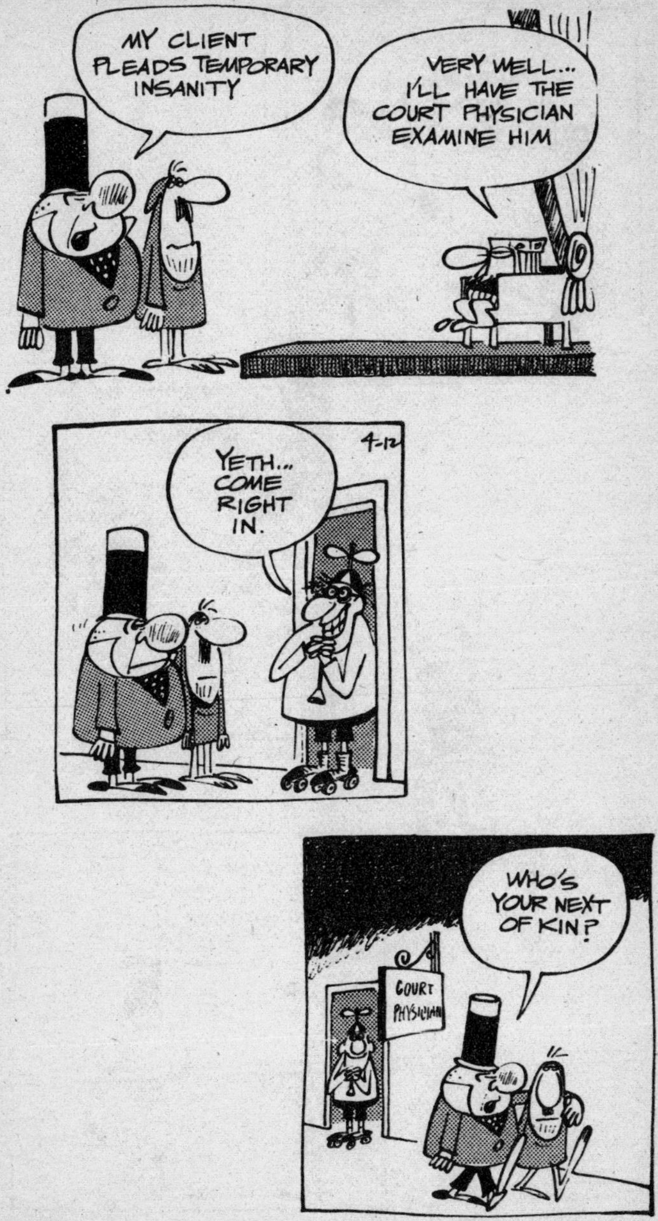
MY CLIENT PLEADS TEMPORARY INSANITY
VERY WELL... I'LL HAVE THE COURT PHYSICIAN EXAMINE HIM
4-12
YETH... COME RIGHT IN.
COURT PHYSICIAN
WHO'S YOUR NEXT OF KIN?

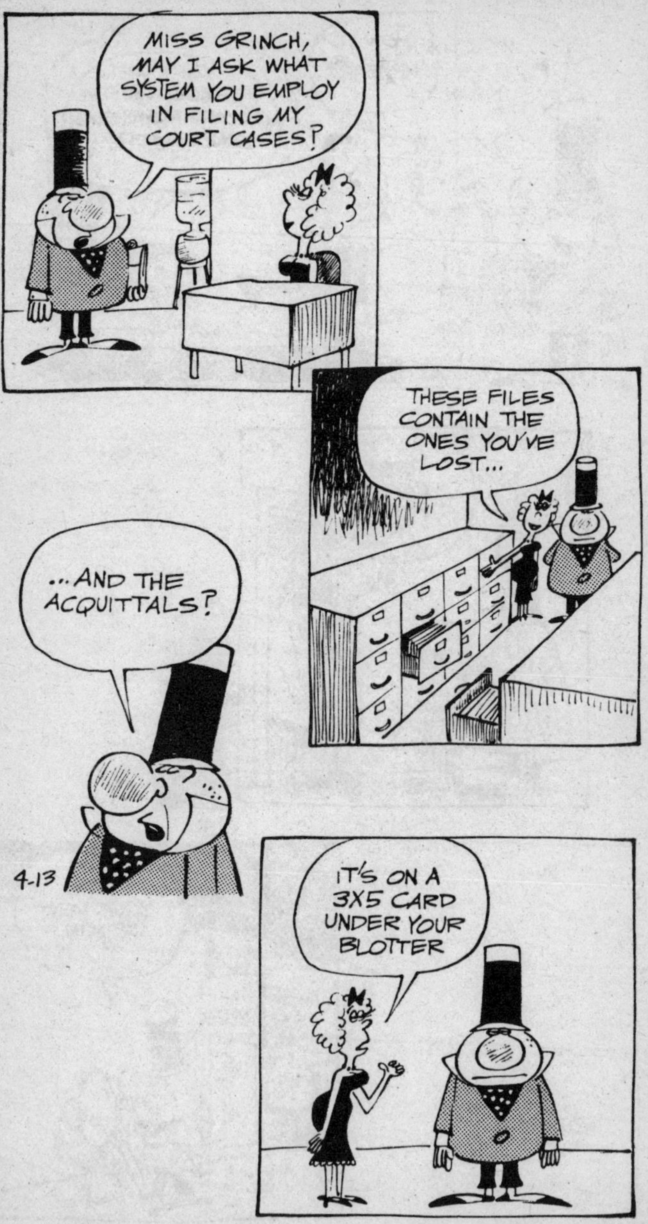
MISS GRINCH, MAY I ASK WHAT SYSTEM YOU EMPLOY IN FILING MY COURT CASES?
THESE FILES CONTAIN THE ONES YOU'VE LOST...
...AND THE ACQUITTALS?
4-13
IT'S ON A 3X5 CARD UNDER YOUR BLOTTER

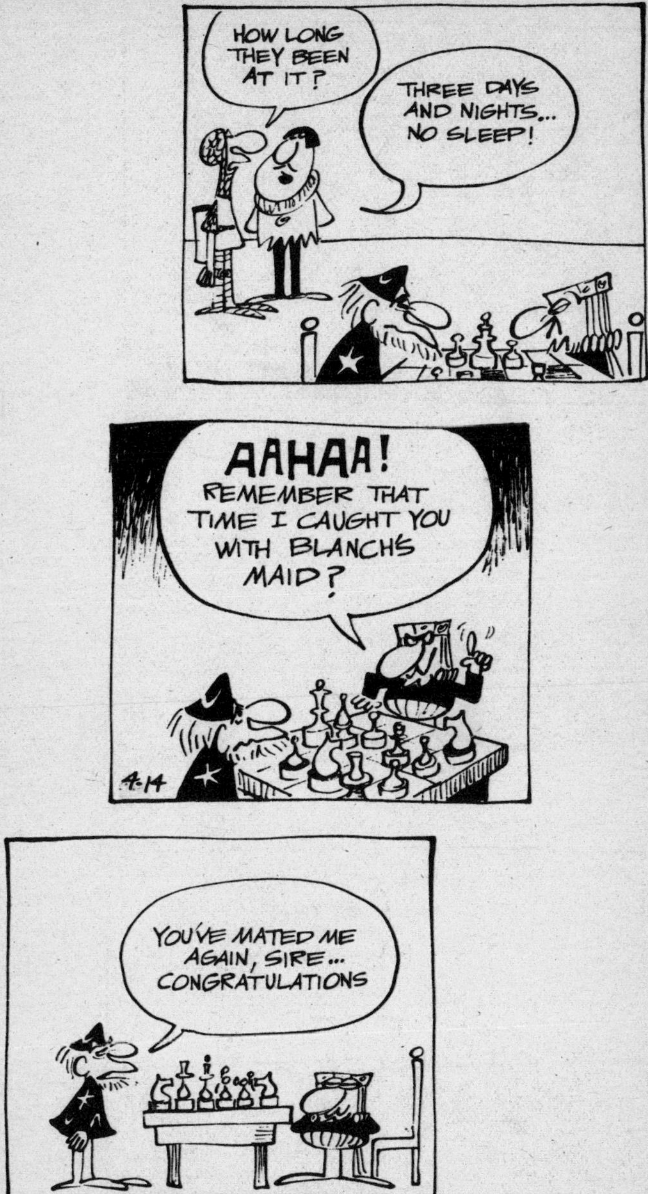
HOW LONG THEY BEEN AT IT?
THREE DAYS AND NIGHTS... NO SLEEP!
AAHAA! REMEMBER THAT TIME I CAUGHT YOU WITH BLANCH'S MAID?
4·14
YOU'VE MATED ME AGAIN, SIRE... CONGRATULATIONS

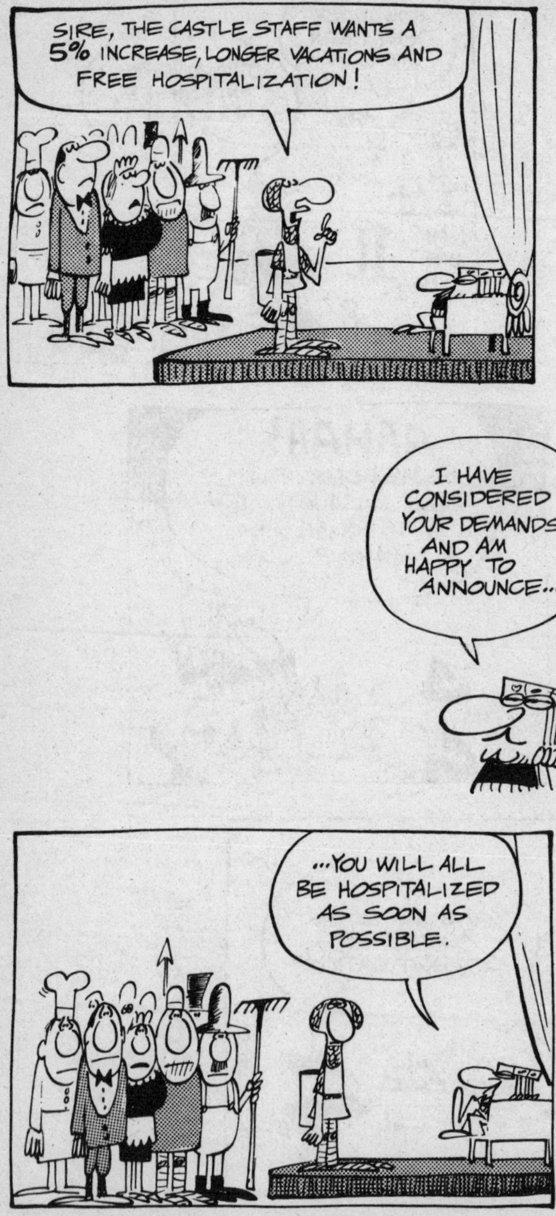
SIRE, THE CASTLE STAFF WANTS A 5% INCREASE, LONGER VACATIONS AND FREE HOSPITALIZATION!
I HAVE CONSIDERED YOUR DEMANDS, AND AM HAPPY TO ANNOUNCE...
4-16
...YOU WILL ALL BE HOSPITALIZED AS SOON AS POSSIBLE.

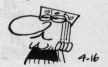

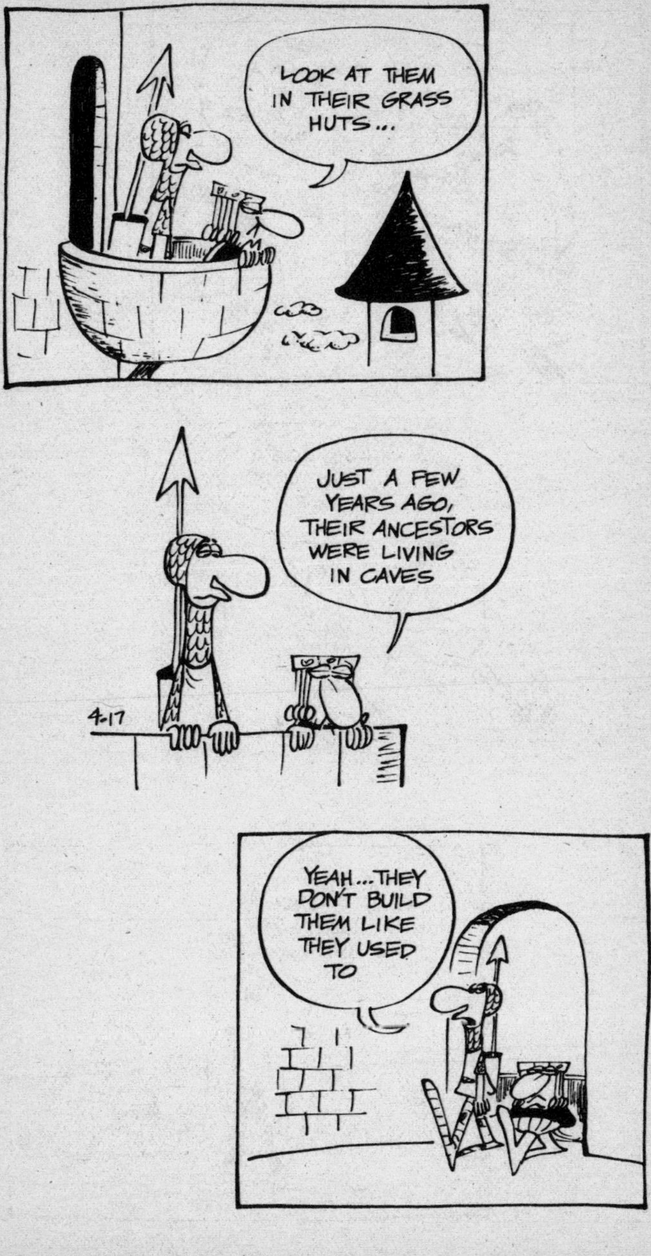
LOOK AT THEM IN THEIR GRASS HUTS...
JUST A FEW YEARS AGO, THEIR ANCESTORS WERE LIVING IN CAVES
4-17
YEAH...THEY DON'T BUILD THEM LIKE THEY USED TO

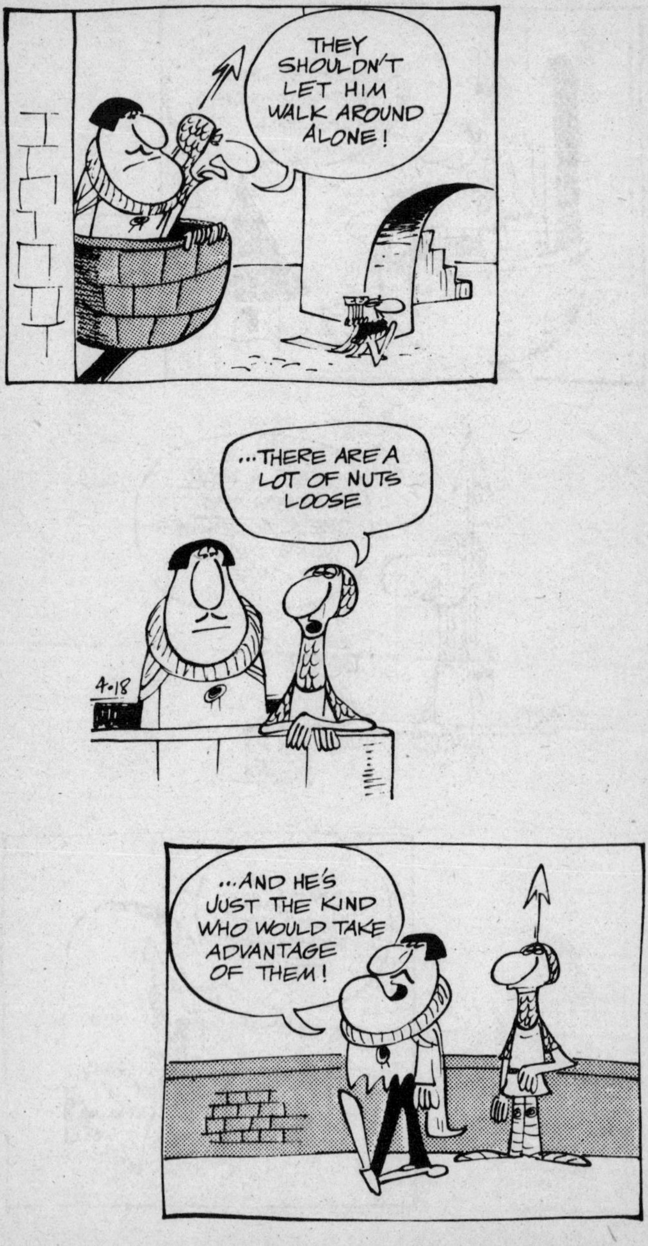
THEY SHOULDN'T LET HIM WALK AROUND ALONE!
...THERE ARE A LOT OF NUTS LOOSE
4•18
...AND HE'S JUST THE KIND WHO WOULD TAKE ADVANTAGE OF THEM!

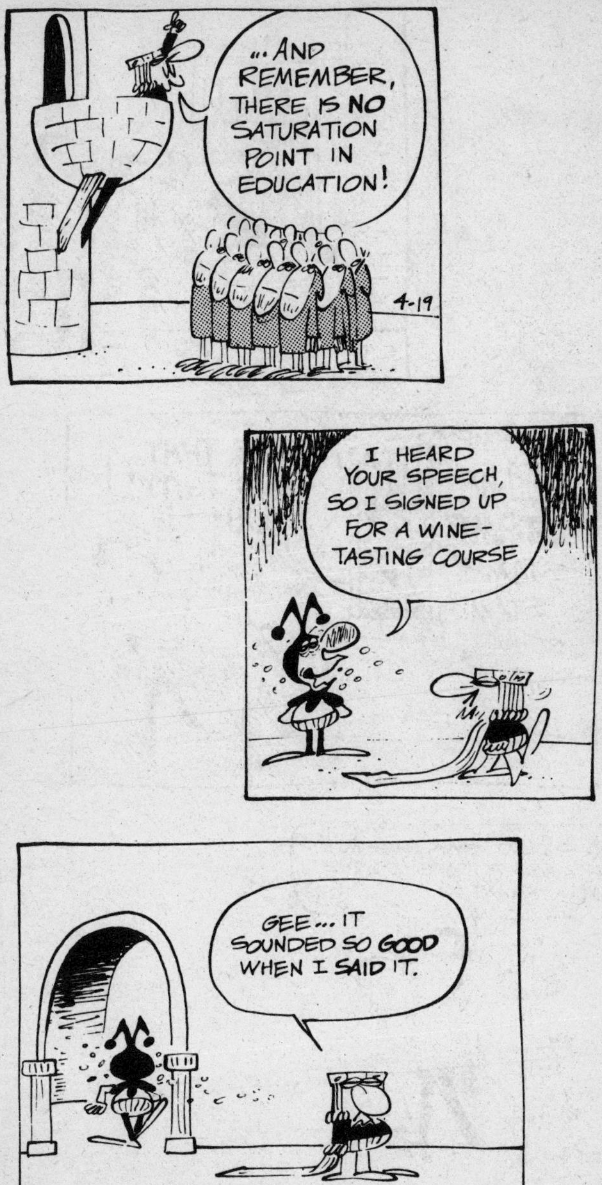

...AND REMEMBER, THERE IS NO SATURATION POINT IN EDUCATION!
4-19
I HEARD YOUR SPEECH, SO I SIGNED UP FOR A WINE-TASTING COURSE
GEE... IT SOUNDED SO GOOD WHEN I SAID IT.

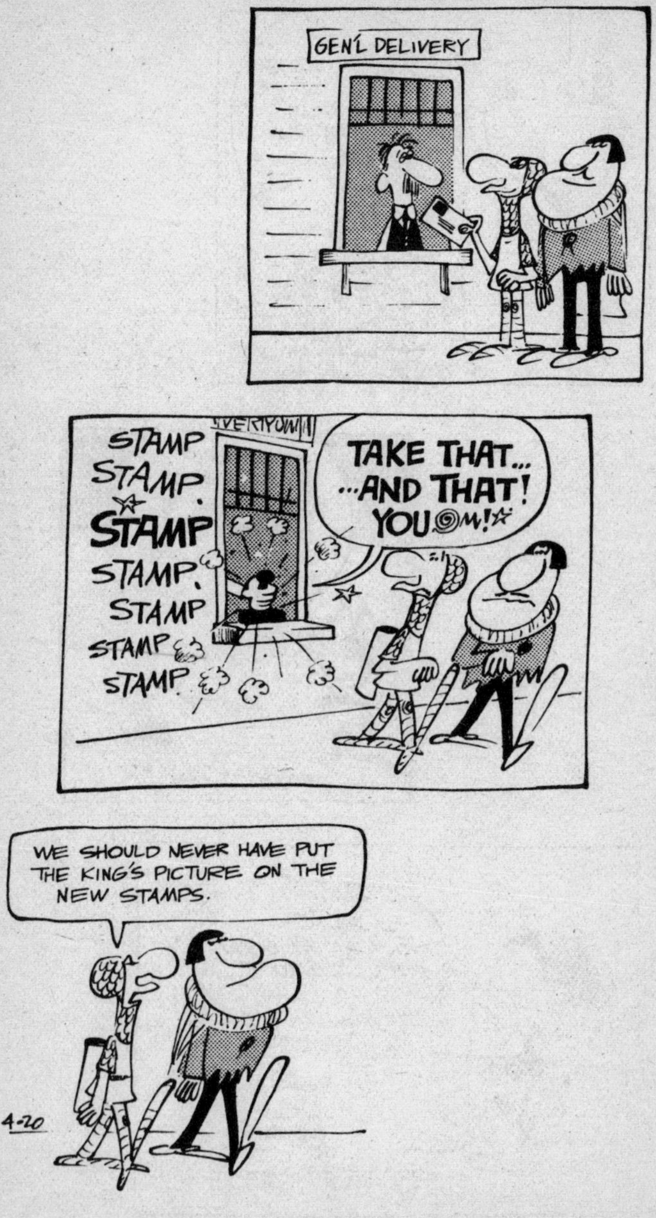
GEN'L DELIVERY
STAMP STAMP STAMP STAMP STAMP STAMP STAMP
TAKE THAT... ...AND THAT! YOU
WE SHOULD NEVER HAVE PUT THE KING'S PICTURE ON THE NEW STAMPS.
4-20

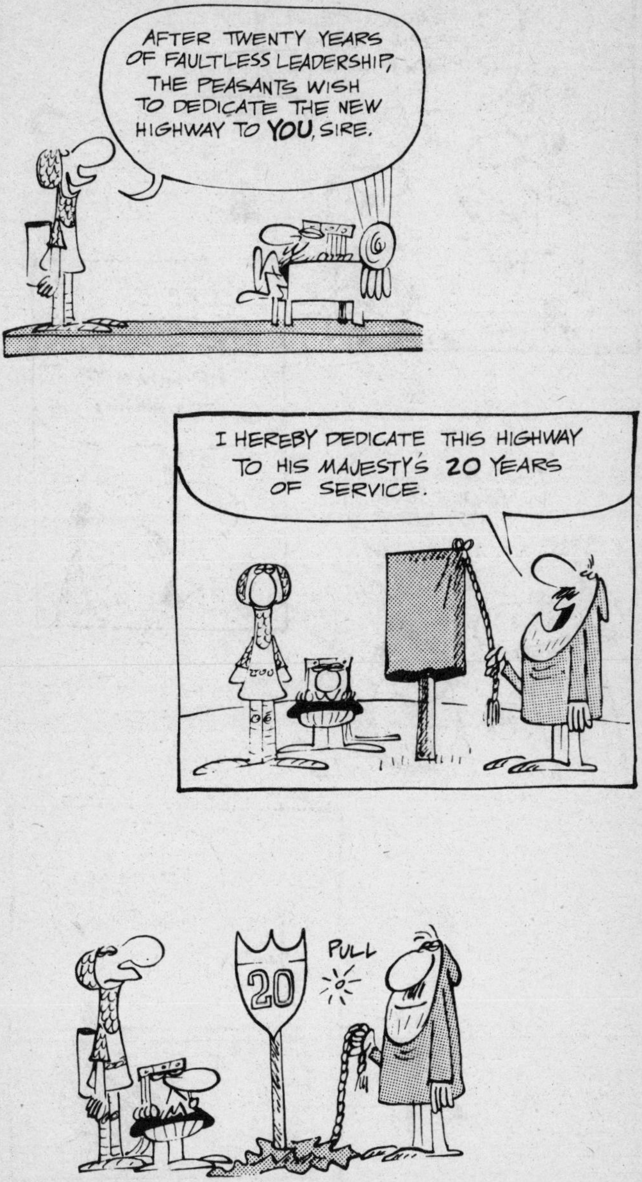
AFTER TWENTY YEARS OF FAULTLESS LEADERSHIP, THE PEASANTS WISH TO DEDICATE THE NEW HIGHWAY TO YOU, SIRE.
I HEREBY DEDICATE THIS HIGHWAY TO HIS MAJESTY'S 20 YEARS OF SERVICE.
20
PULL

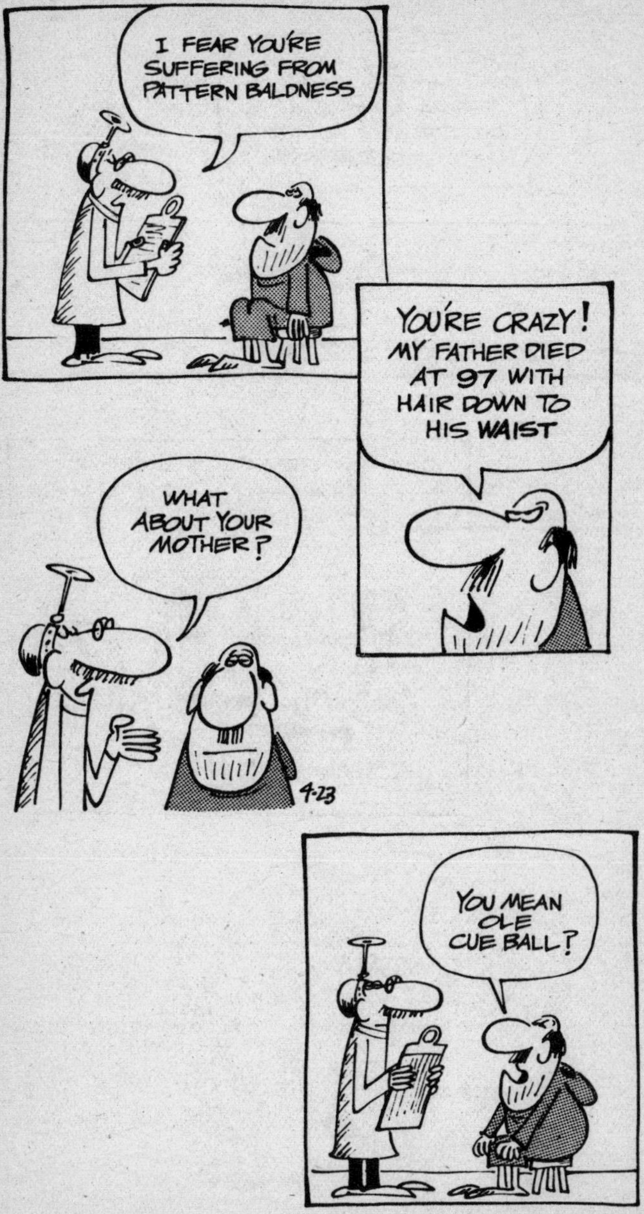
I FEAR YOU'RE SUFFERING FROM PATTERN BALDNESS
YOU'RE CRAZY! MY FATHER DIED AT 97 WITH HAIR DOWN TO HIS WAIST
WHAT ABOUT YOUR MOTHER?
4-23
YOU MEAN OLE CUE BALL?

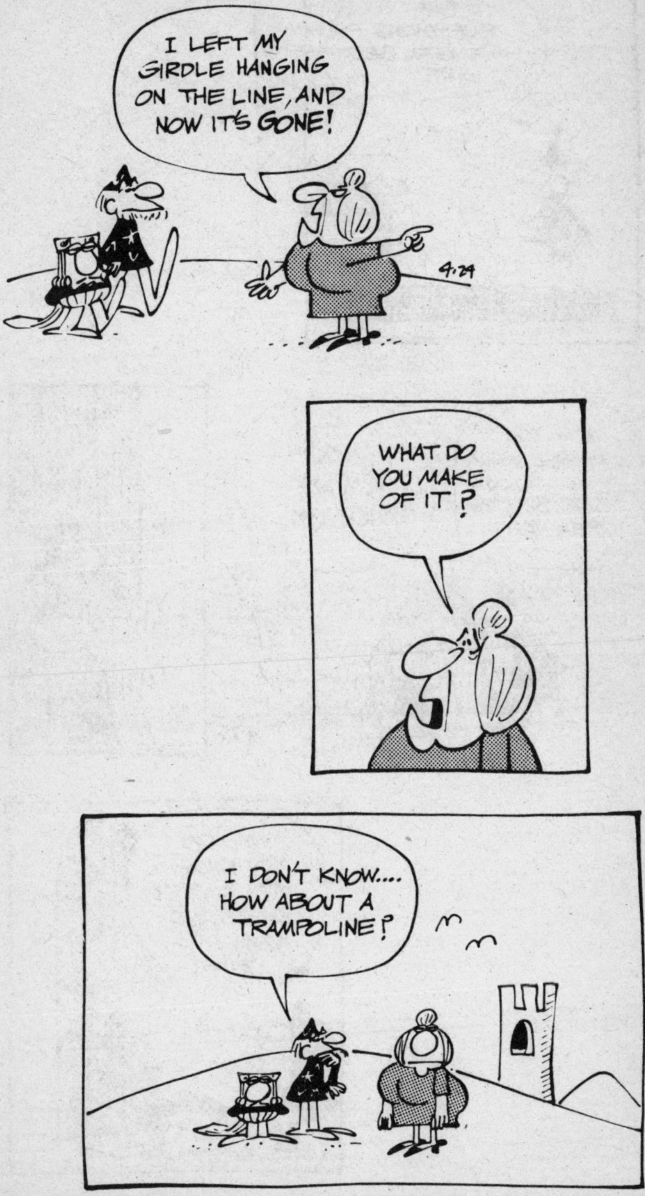
I LEFT MY GIRDLE HANGING ON THE LINE, AND NOW IT'S GONE!
4.24
WHAT DO YOU MAKE OF IT?
I DON'T KNOW.... HOW ABOUT A TRAMPOLINE?

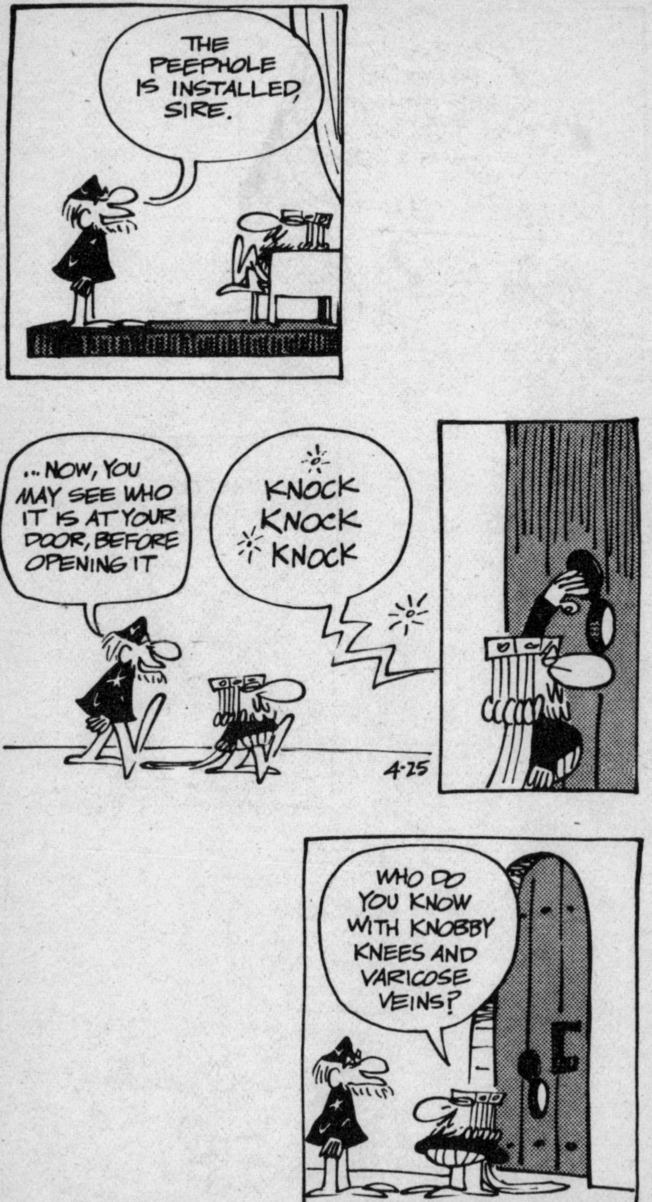
THE PEEPHOLE IS INSTALLED, SIRE.
... NOW, YOU MAY SEE WHO IT IS AT YOUR DOOR, BEFORE OPENING IT
KNOCK KNOCK KNOCK
4-25
WHO DO YOU KNOW WITH KNOBBY KNEES AND VARICOSE VEINS?

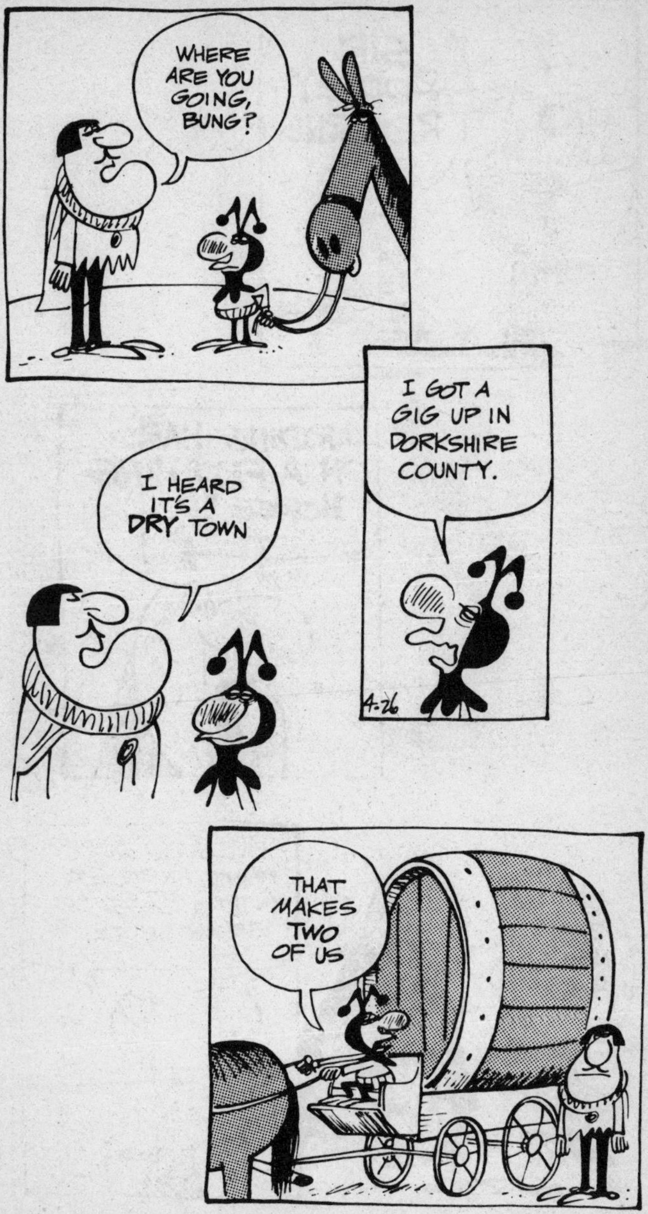
WHERE ARE YOU GOING, BUNG?
I GOT A GIG UP IN DORKSHIRE COUNTY.
I HEARD IT'S A DRY TOWN
THAT MAKES TWO OF US
4-26

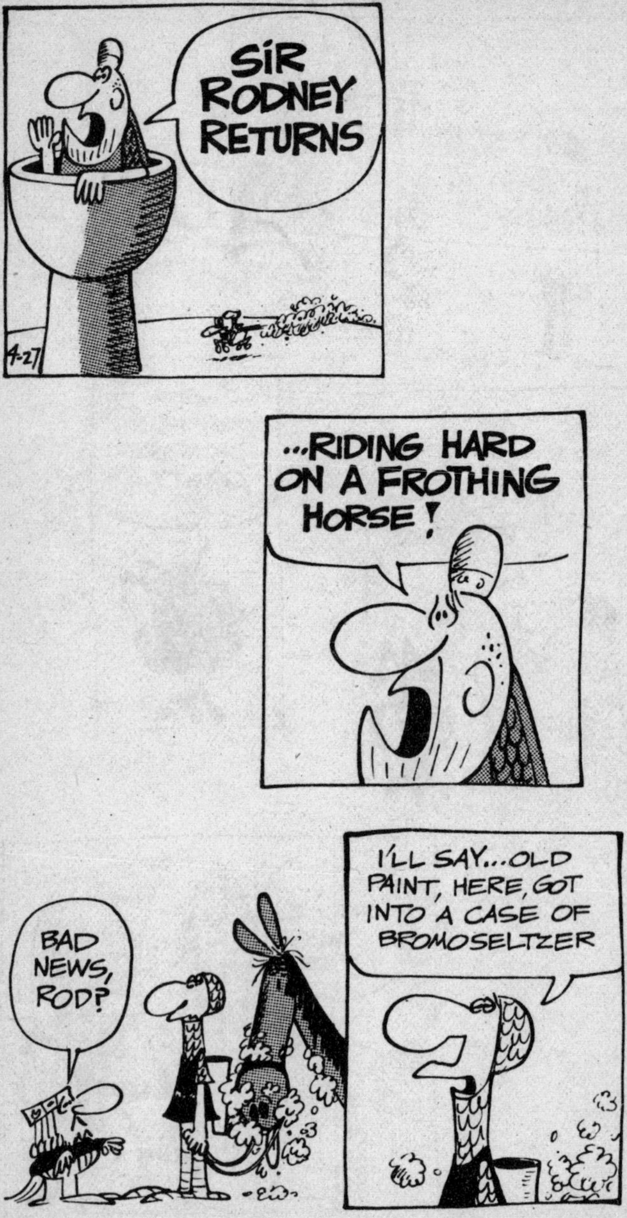
SIR RODNEY RETURNS
4-27
...RIDING HARD ON A FROTHING HORSE!
BAD NEWS, ROD?
I'LL SAY...OLD PAINT, HERE, GOT INTO A CASE OF BROMOSELTZER

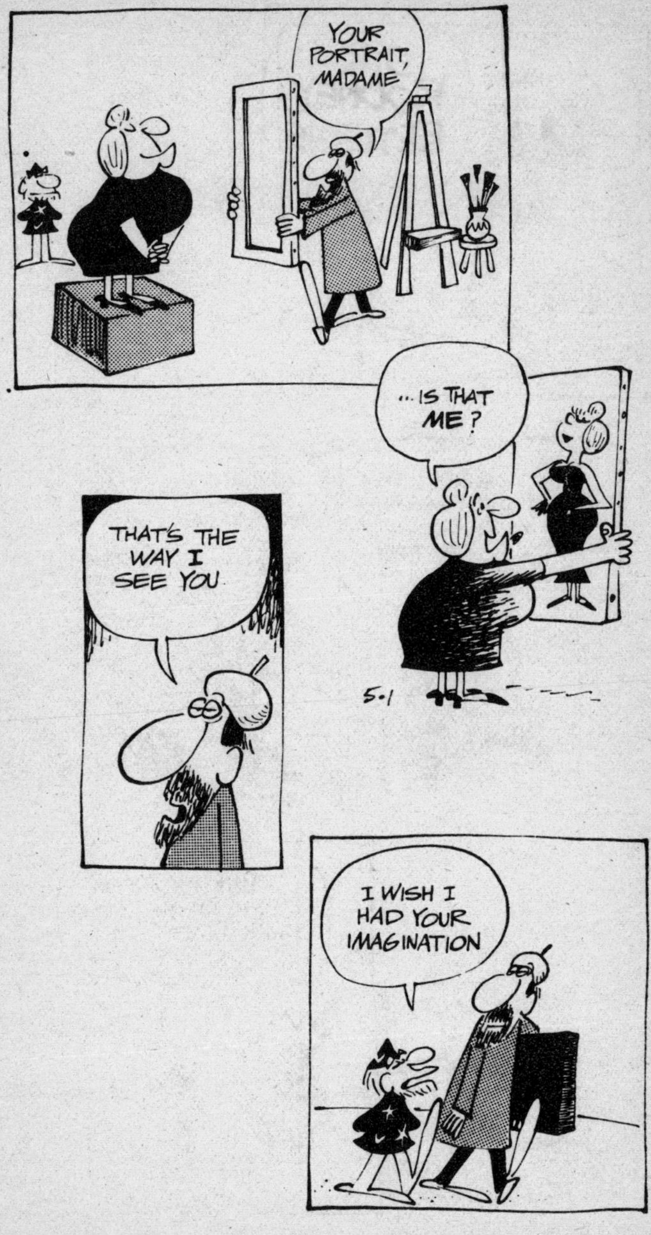
YOUR PORTRAIT, MADAME
...IS THAT ME?
5-1
THAT'S THE WAY I SEE YOU
I WISH I HAD YOUR IMAGINATION

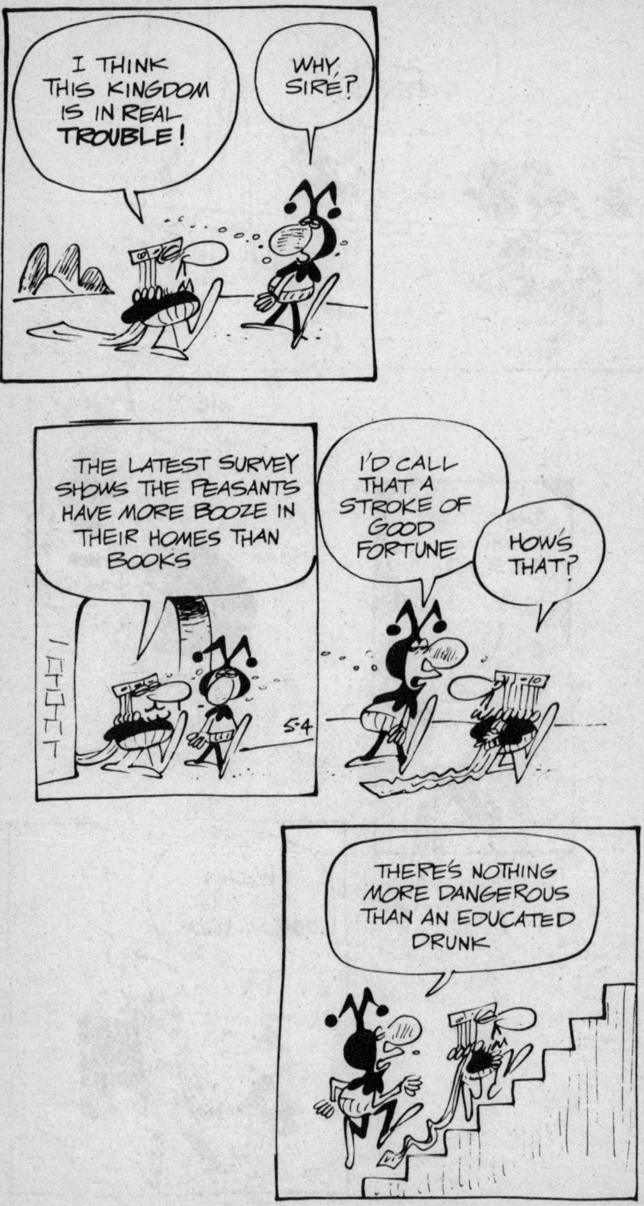
I THINK THIS KINGDOM IS IN REAL TROUBLE!
WHY, SIRE?
THE LATEST SURVEY SHOWS THE PEASANTS HAVE MORE BOOZE IN THEIR HOMES THAN BOOKS
5-4
I'D CALL THAT A STROKE OF GOOD FORTUNE
HOW'S THAT?
THERE'S NOTHING MORE DANGEROUS THAN AN EDUCATED DRUNK

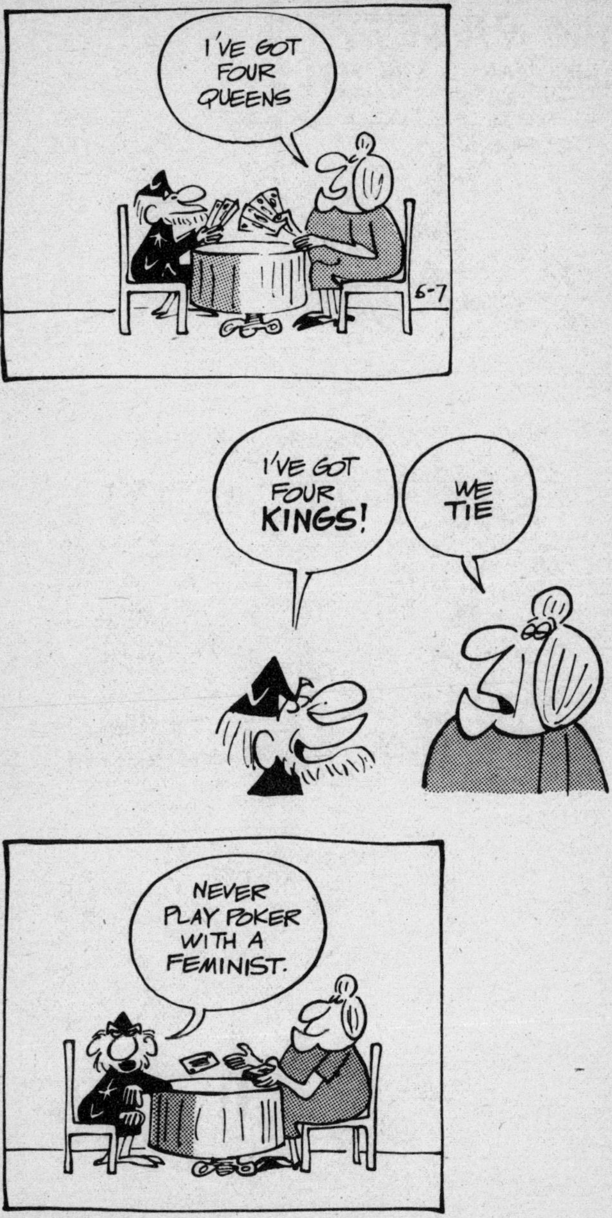
I'VE GOT FOUR QUEENS
6-7
I'VE GOT FOUR KINGS!
WE TIE
NEVER PLAY POKER WITH A FEMINIST.

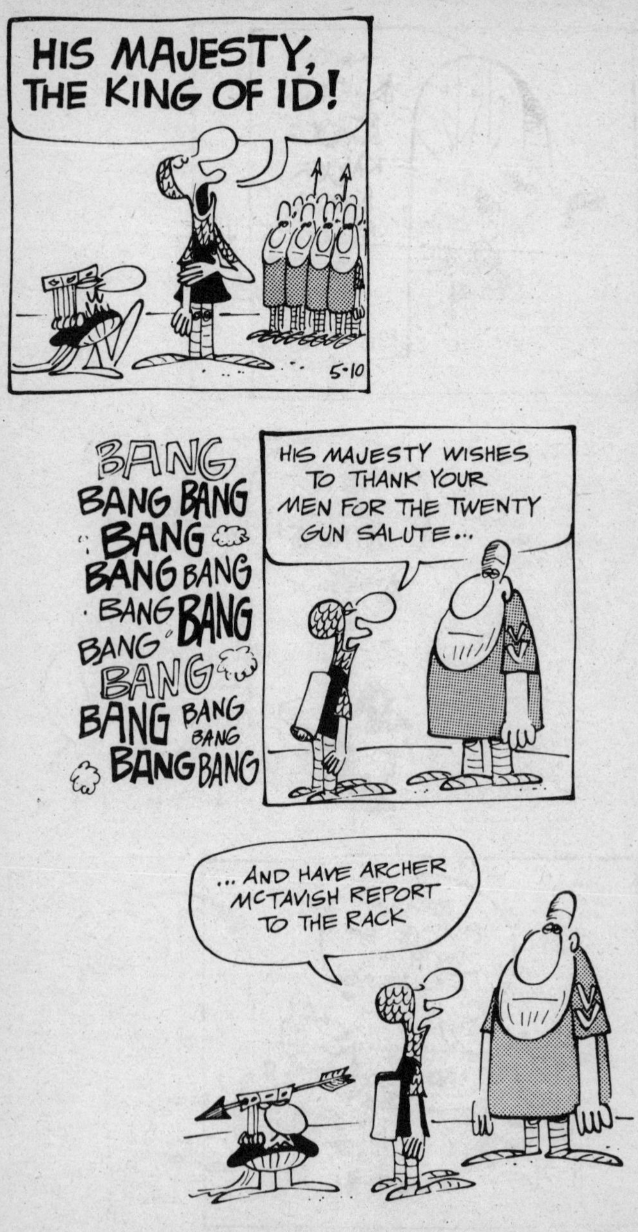

HIS MAJESTY, THE KING OF ID!
5-10
BANG
BANG BANG
BANG
BANG BANG
BANG BANG
BANG
BANG
BANG BANG
BANG
BANG BANG
HIS MAJESTY WISHES TO THANK YOUR MEN FOR THE TWENTY GUN SALUTE...
... AND HAVE ARCHER MCTAVISH REPORT TO THE RACK

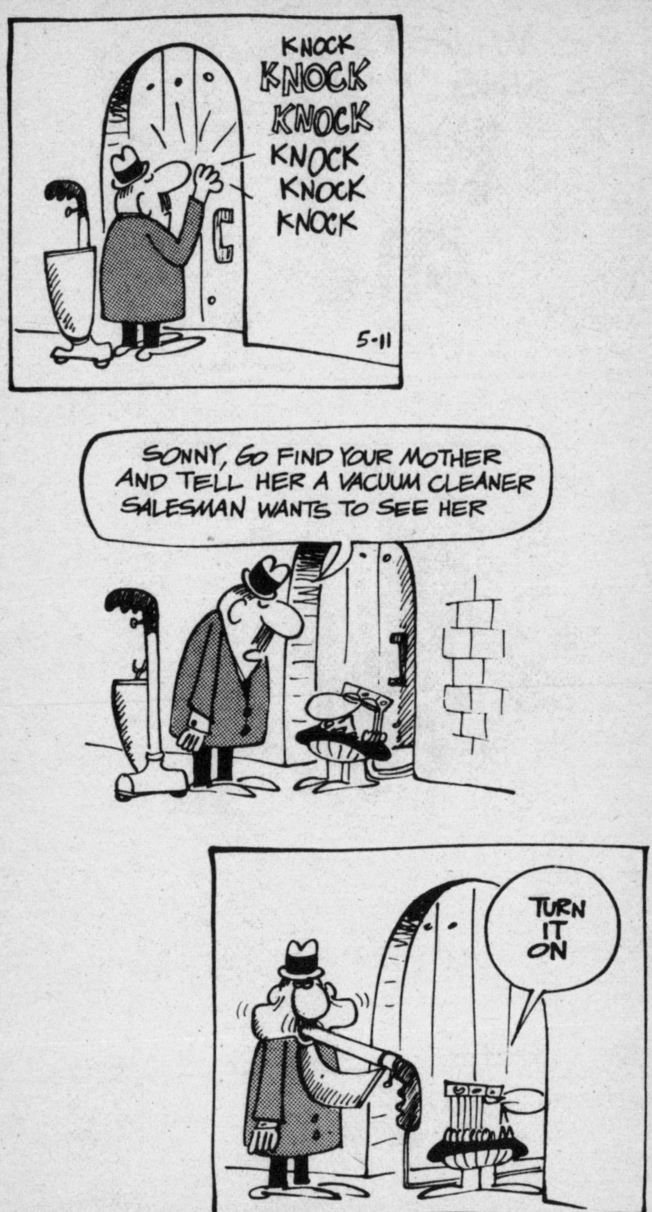
KNOCK
KNOCK
KNOCK
KNOCK
KNOCK
KNOCK
5-11
SONNY, GO FIND YOUR MOTHER AND TELL HER A VACUUM CLEANER SALESMAN WANTS TO SEE HER
TURN IT ON

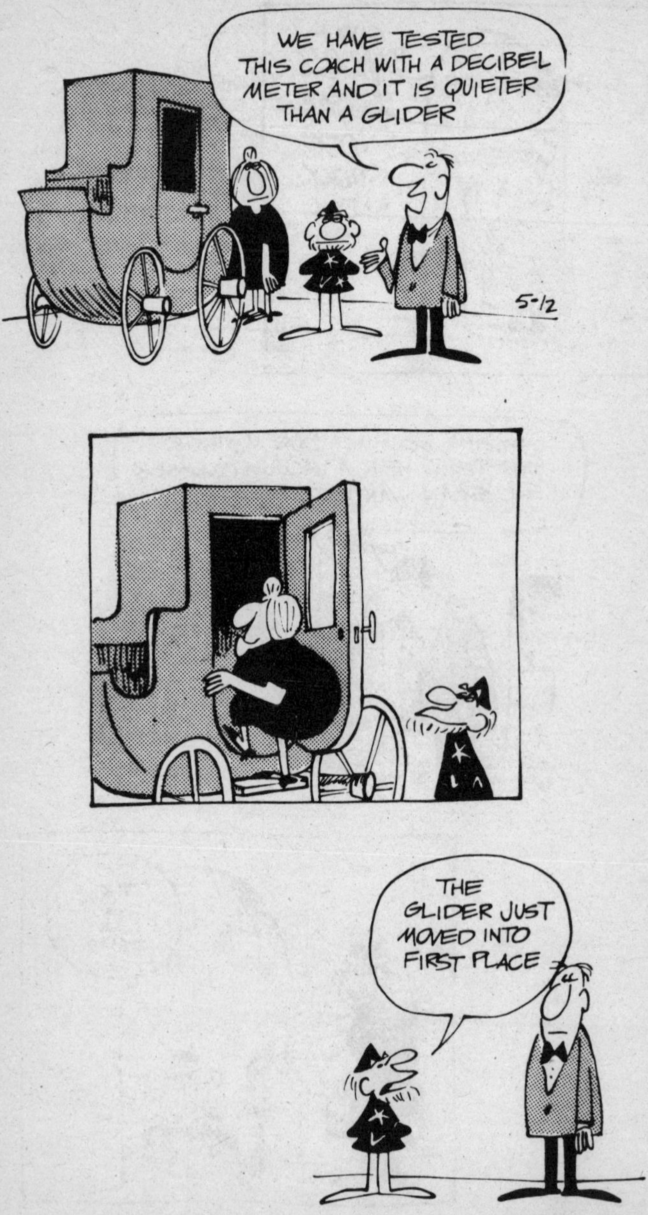
WE HAVE TESTED THIS COACH WITH A DECIBEL METER AND IT IS QUIETER THAN A GLIDER
5-12
THE GLIDER JUST MOVED INTO FIRST PLACE

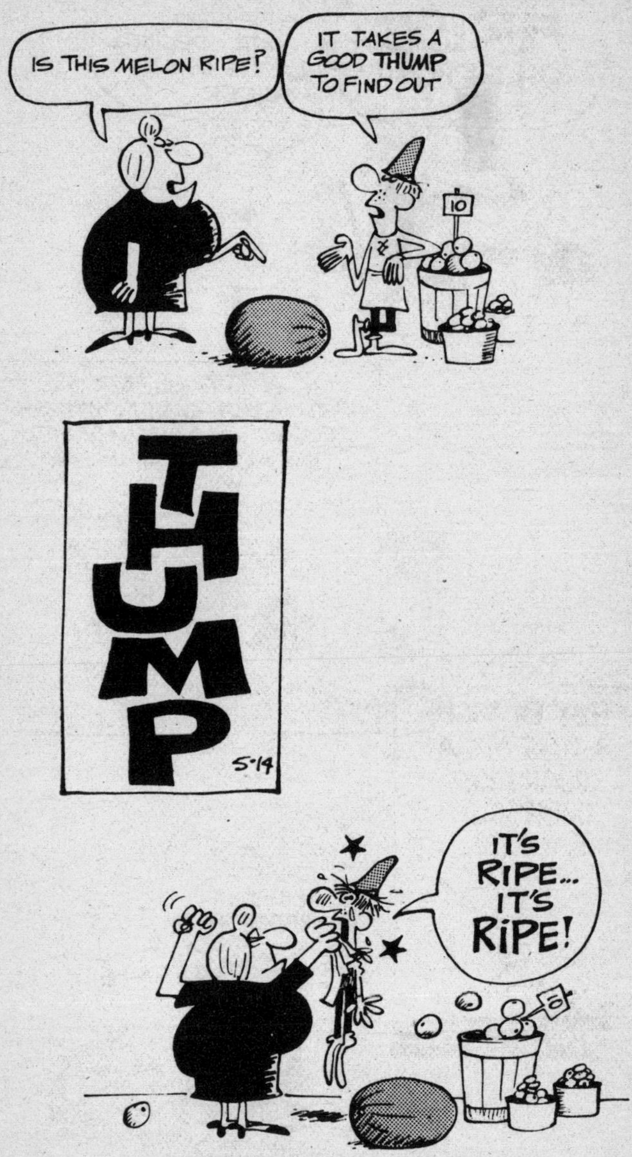
IS THIS MELON RIPE?
IT TAKES A GOOD THUMP TO FIND OUT
10
THUMP
5-14
IT'S RIPE... IT'S RIPE!

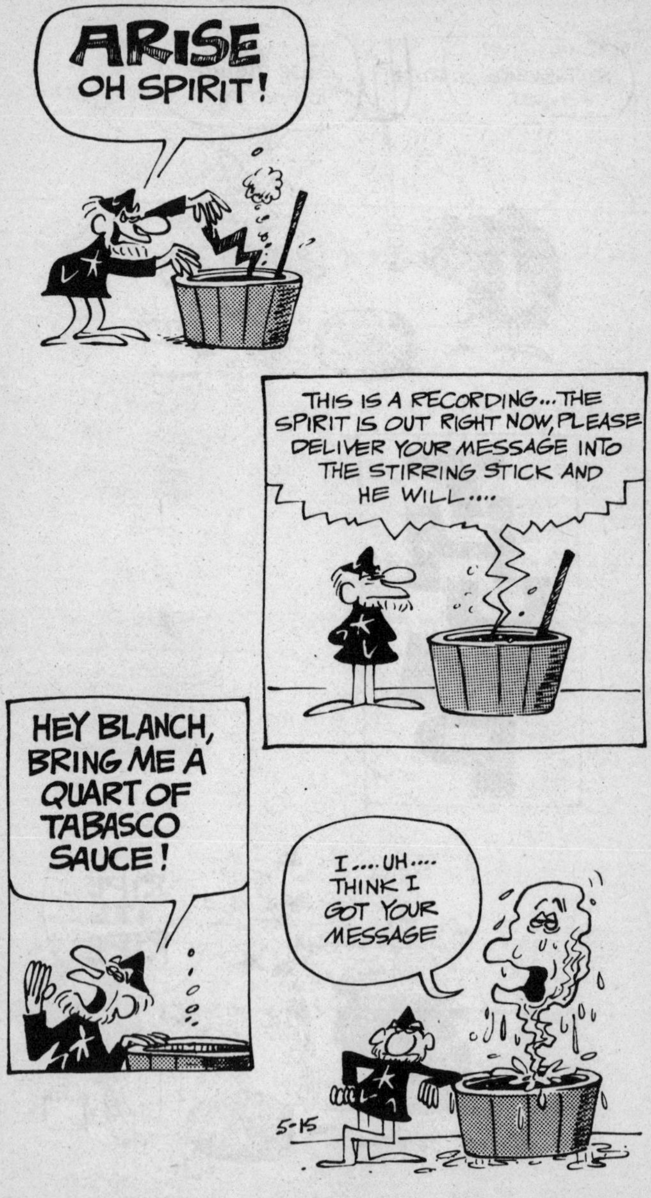
ARISE OH SPIRIT!
THIS IS A RECORDING...THE SPIRIT IS OUT RIGHT NOW, PLEASE DELIVER YOUR MESSAGE INTO THE STIRRING STICK AND HE WILL....
HEY BLANCH, BRING ME A QUART OF TABASCO SAUCE!
I....UH.... THINK I GOT YOUR MESSAGE
5-15

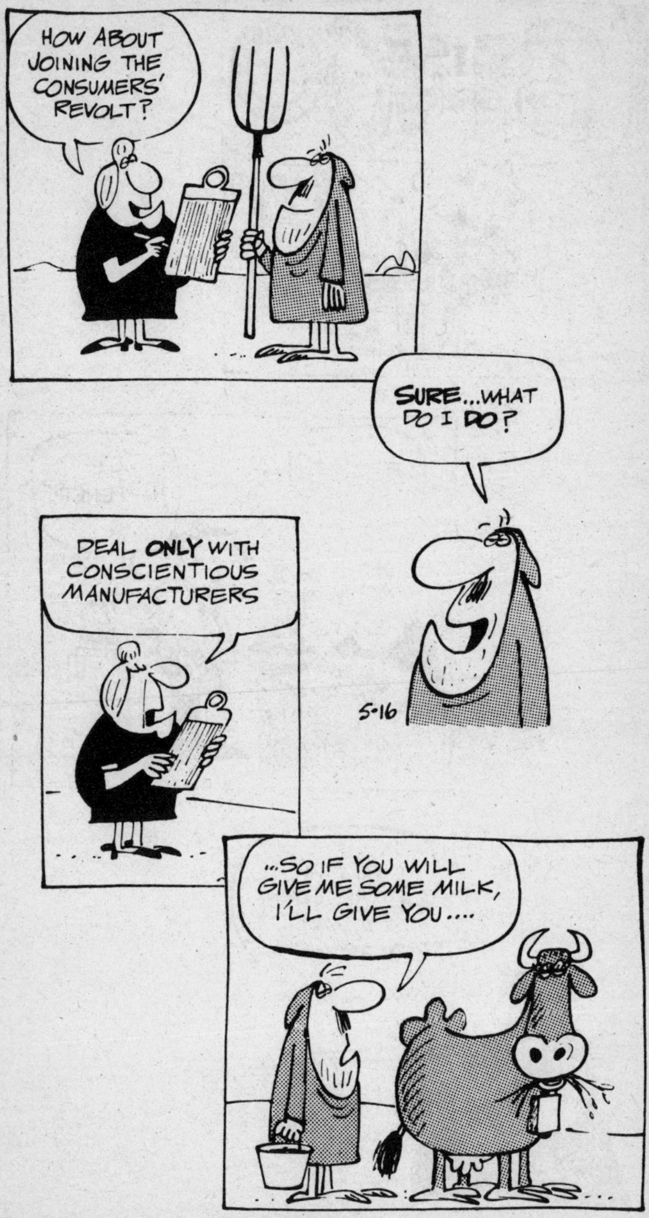
HOW ABOUT JOINING THE CONSUMERS' REVOLT?
SURE...WHAT DO I DO?
DEAL ONLY WITH CONSCIENTIOUS MANUFACTURERS
5-16
...SO IF YOU WILL GIVE ME SOME MILK, I'LL GIVE YOU....

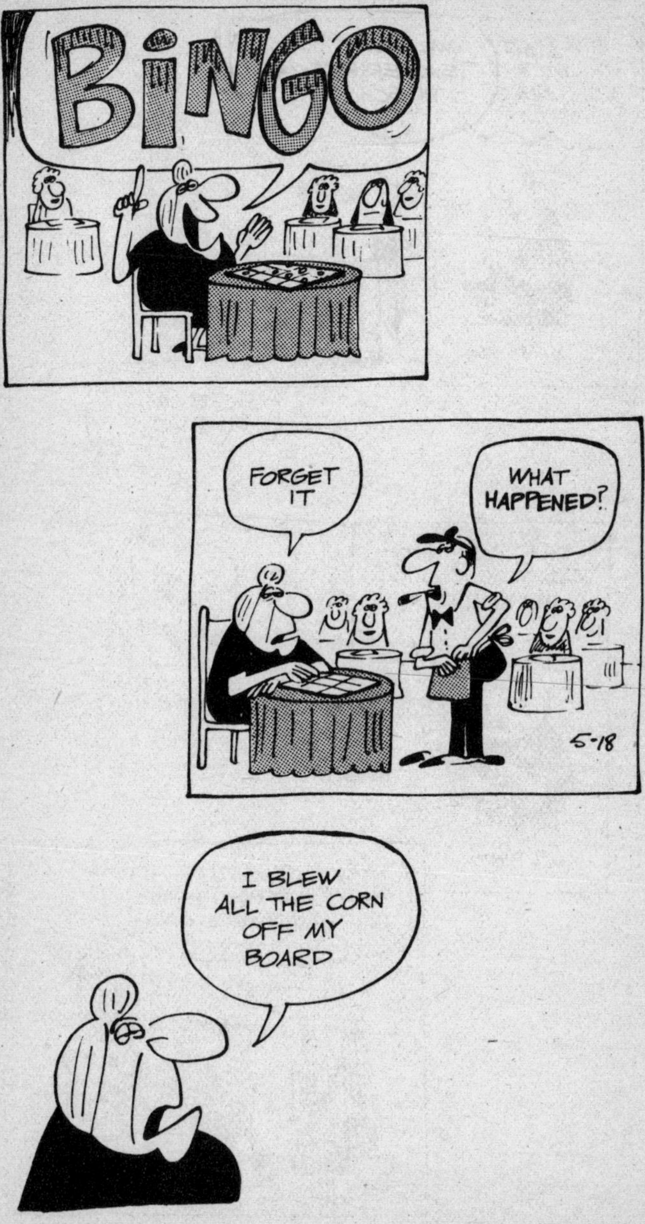
BINGO
FORGET IT
WHAT HAPPENED?
5-18
I BLEW ALL THE CORN OFF MY BOARD

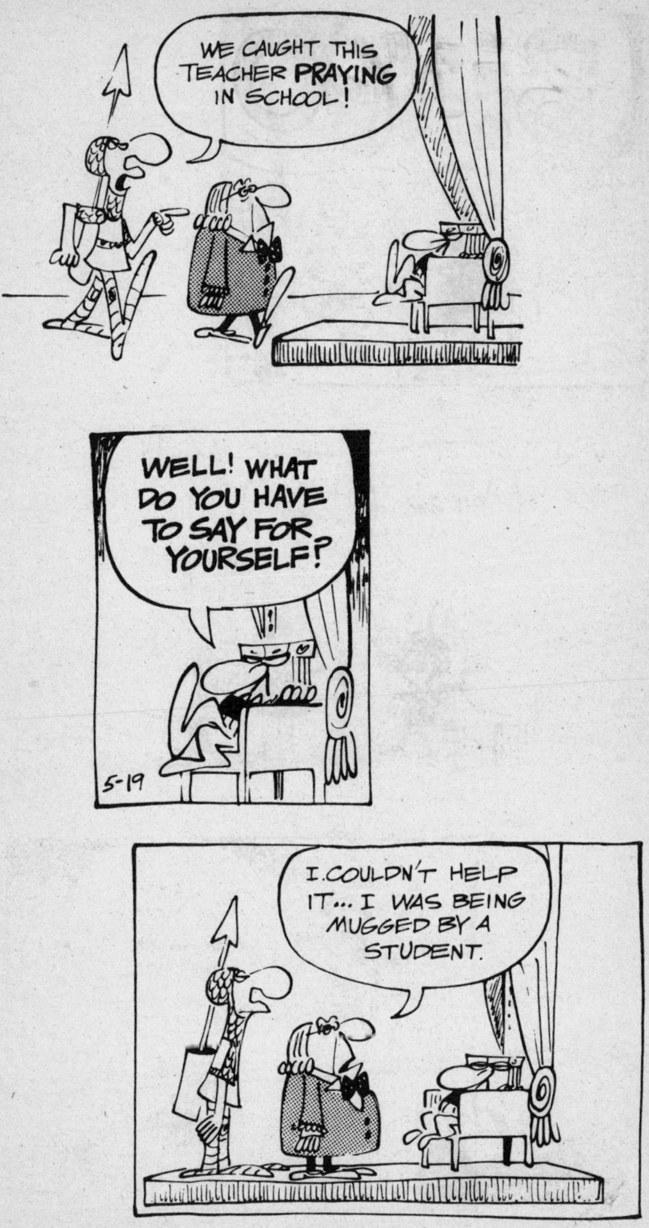
WE CAUGHT THIS TEACHER PRAYING IN SCHOOL!
WELL! WHAT DO YOU HAVE TO SAY FOR YOURSELF?
5-19
I. COULDN'T HELP IT... I WAS BEING MUGGED BY A STUDENT.

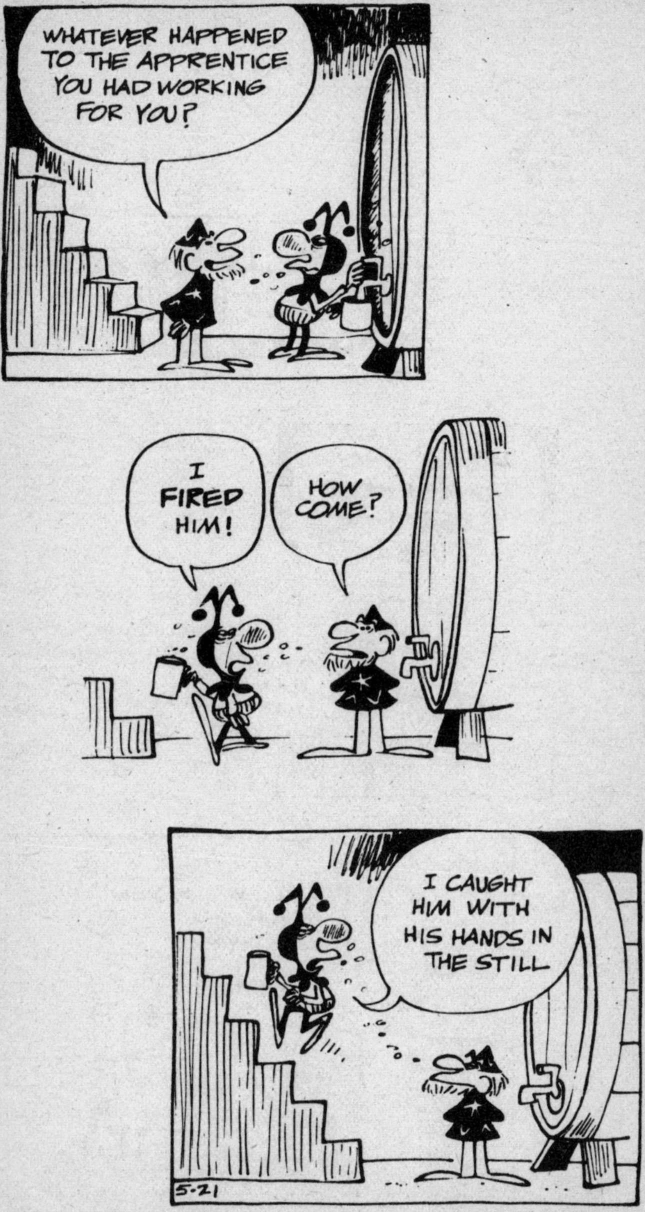
WHATEVER HAPPENED TO THE APPRENTICE YOU HAD WORKING FOR YOU?
I FIRED HIM!
HOW COME?
I CAUGHT HIM WITH HIS HANDS IN THE STILL
5-21

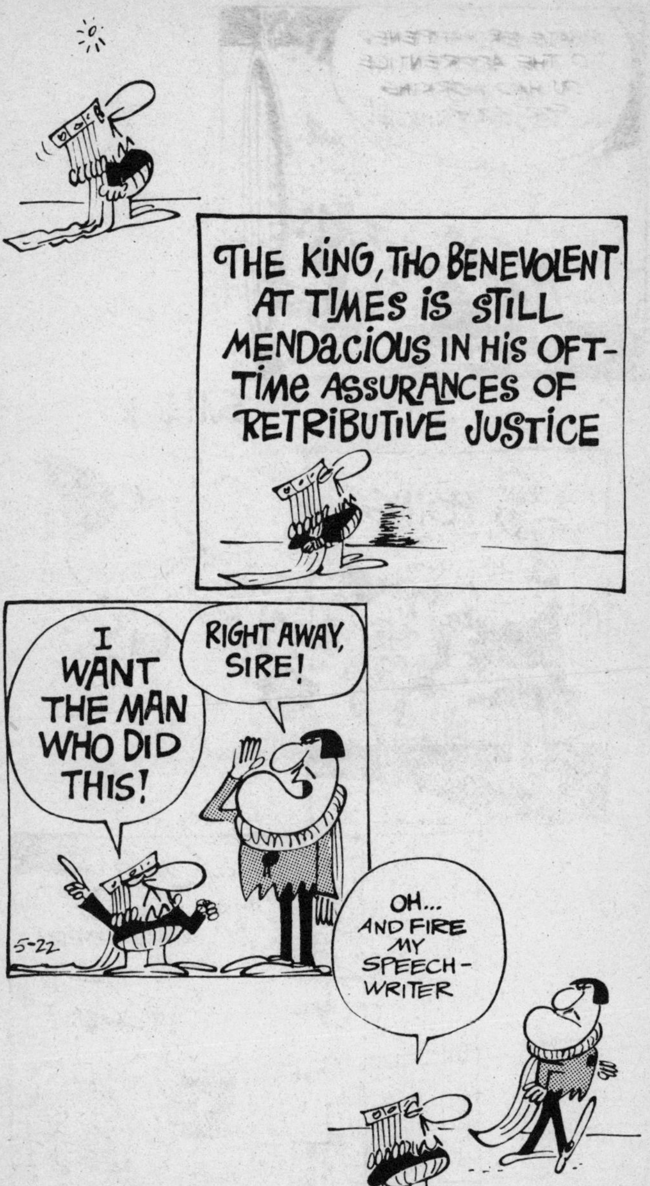
THE KING, THO BENEVOLENT AT TIMES IS STILL MENDACIOUS IN HIS OFT-TIME ASSURANCES OF RETRIBUTIVE JUSTICE
I WANT THE MAN WHO DID THIS!
RIGHT AWAY, SIRE!
5-22
OH... AND FIRE MY SPEECH-WRITER

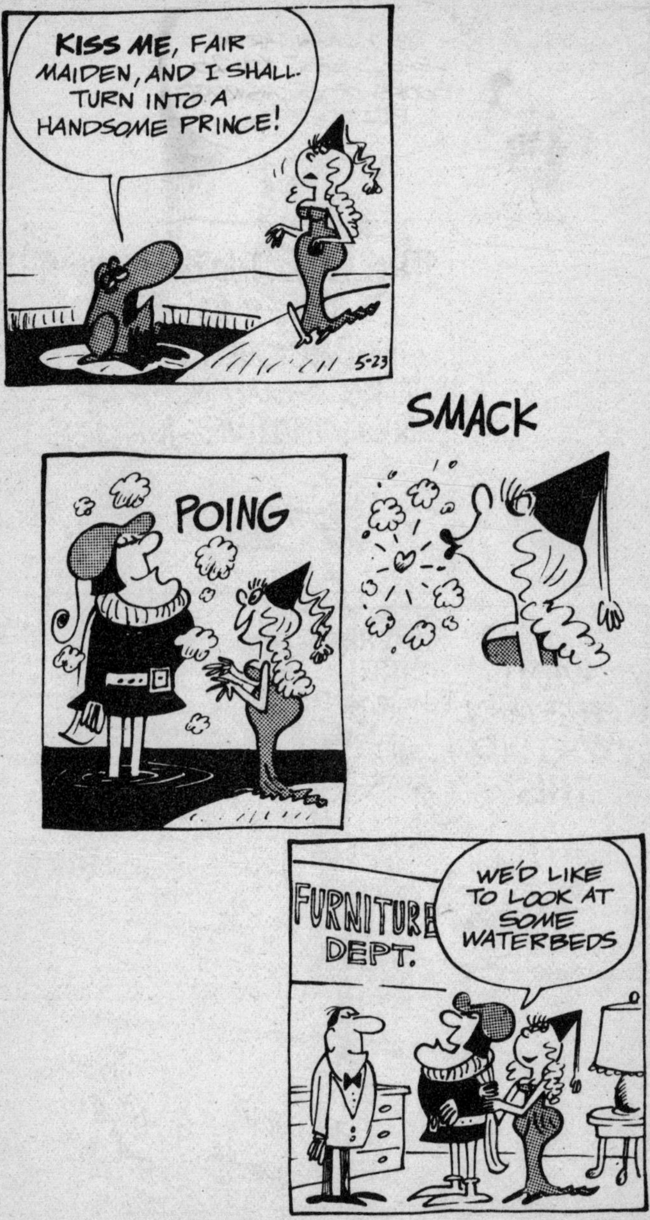
KISS ME, FAIR MAIDEN, AND I SHALL TURN INTO A HANDSOME PRINCE!
5-23
SMACK
POING
FURNITURE DEPT.
WE'D LIKE TO LOOK AT SOME WATERBEDS

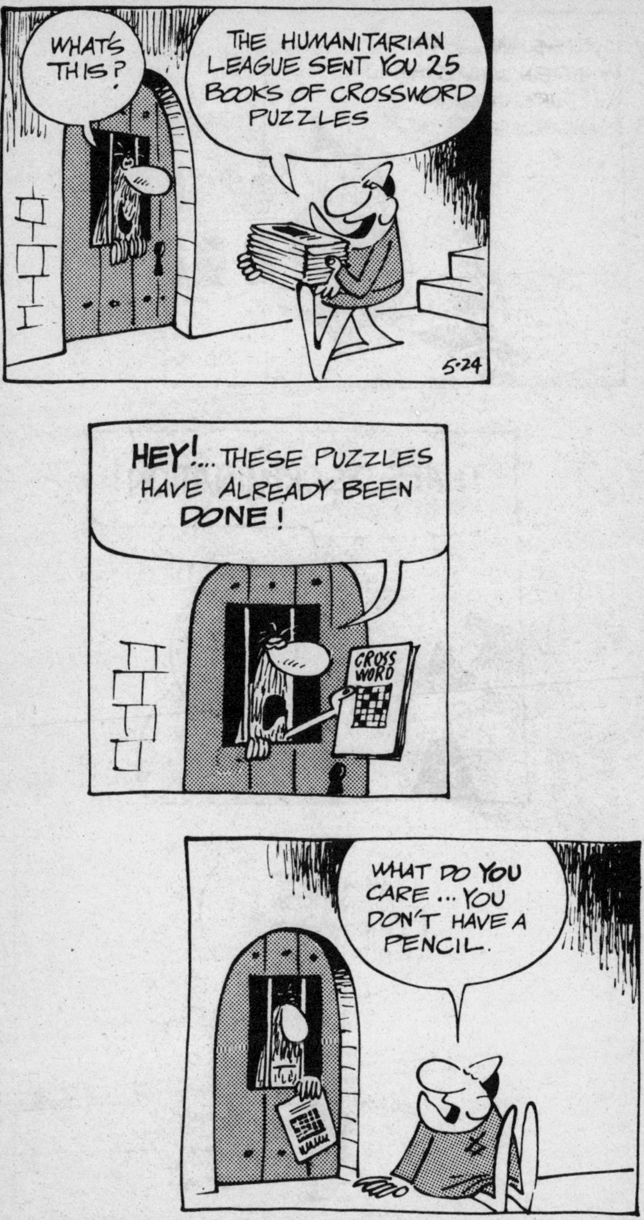
WHAT'S THIS?
THE HUMANITARIAN LEAGUE SENT YOU 25 BOOKS OF CROSSWORD PUZZLES
5-24
HEY!... THESE PUZZLES HAVE ALREADY BEEN DONE!
CROSS WORD
WHAT DO YOU CARE ... YOU DON'T HAVE A PENCIL.

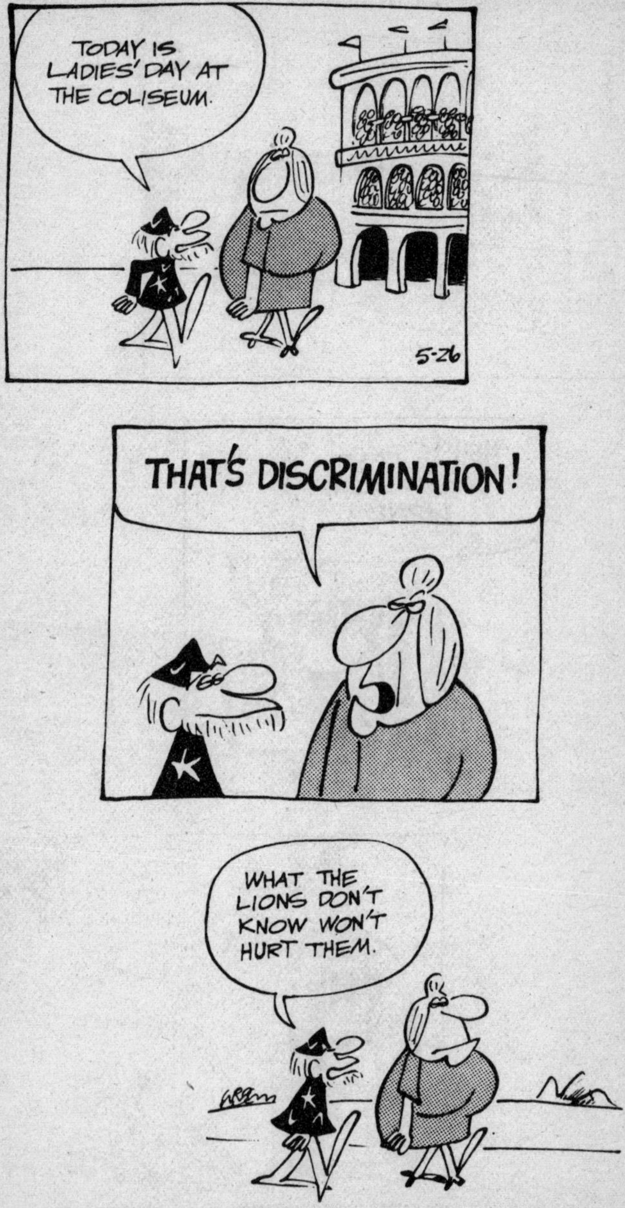
TODAY IS LADIES' DAY AT THE COLISEUM.
5-26
THAT'S DISCRIMINATION!
WHAT THE LIONS DON'T KNOW WON'T HURT THEM.

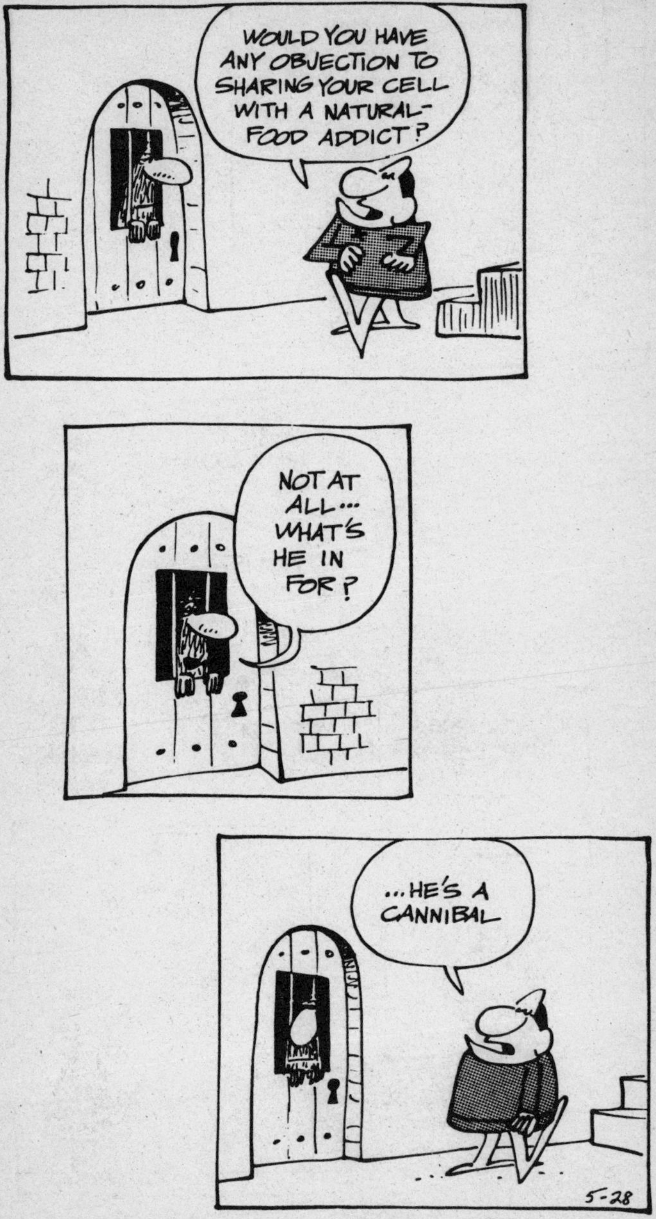
WOULD YOU HAVE ANY OBJECTION TO SHARING YOUR CELL WITH A NATURAL-FOOD ADDICT?
NOT AT ALL... WHAT'S HE IN FOR?
...HE'S A CANNIBAL
5-28

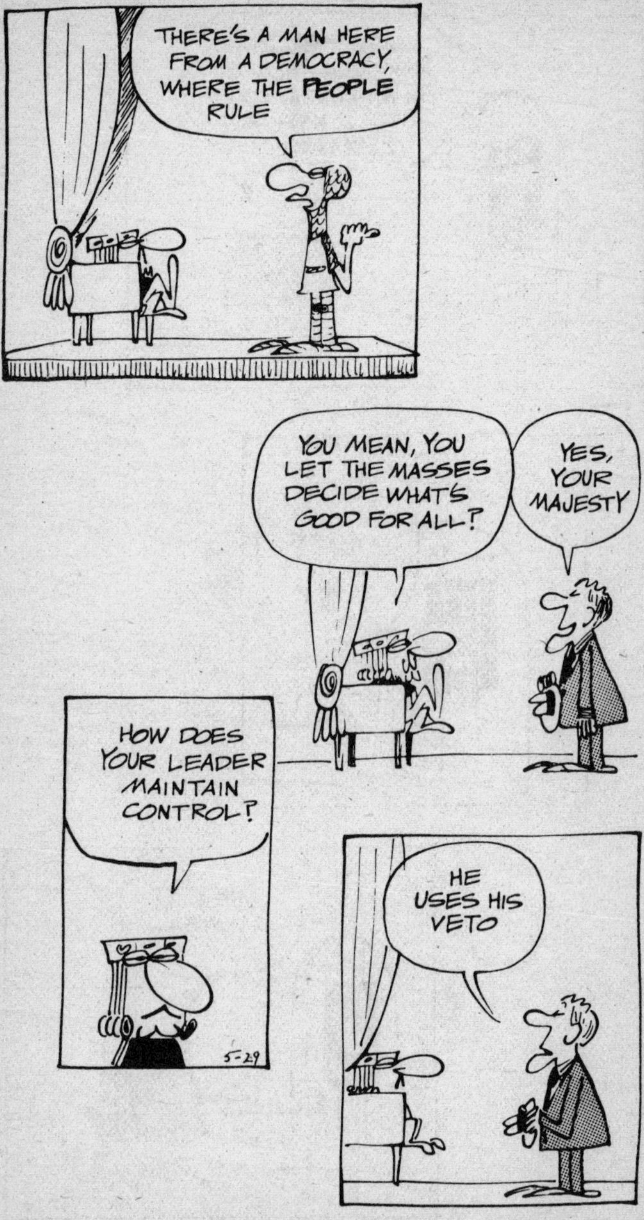
THERE'S A MAN HERE FROM A DEMOCRACY, WHERE THE PEOPLE RULE
YOU MEAN, YOU LET THE MASSES DECIDE WHAT'S GOOD FOR ALL?
YES, YOUR MAJESTY
HOW DOES YOUR LEADER MAINTAIN CONTROL?
HE USES HIS VETO
5-29

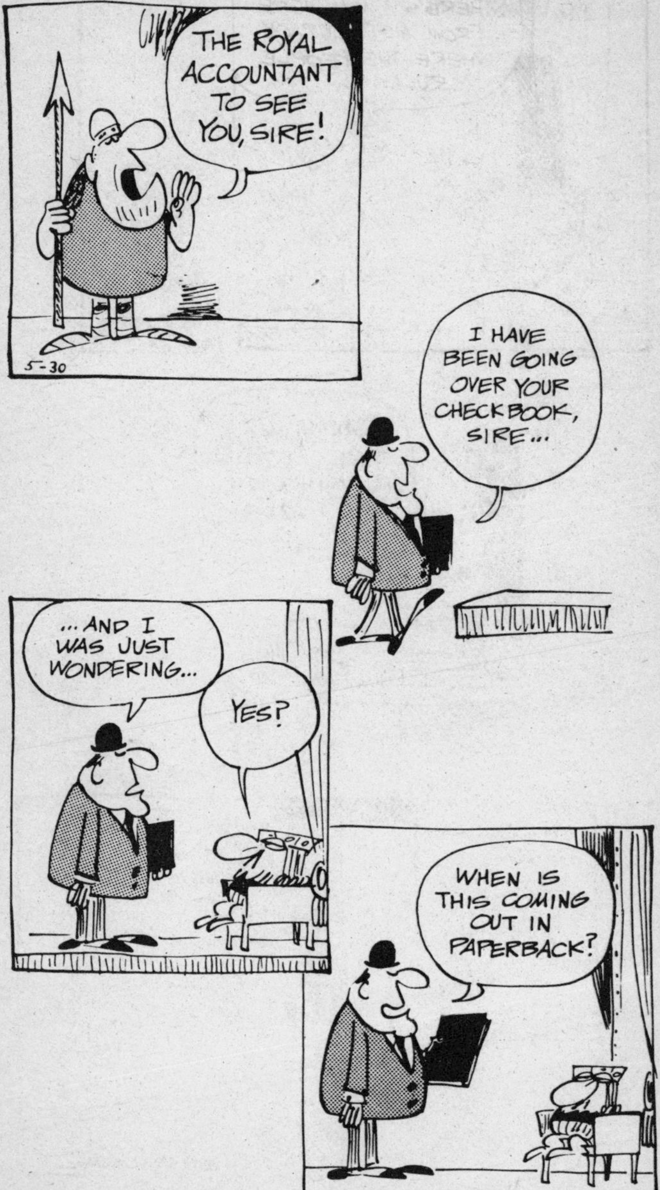
THE ROYAL ACCOUNTANT TO SEE YOU, SIRE!
5-30
I HAVE BEEN GOING OVER YOUR CHECKBOOK, SIRE...
...AND I WAS JUST WONDERING...
YES?
WHEN IS THIS COMING OUT IN PAPERBACK?

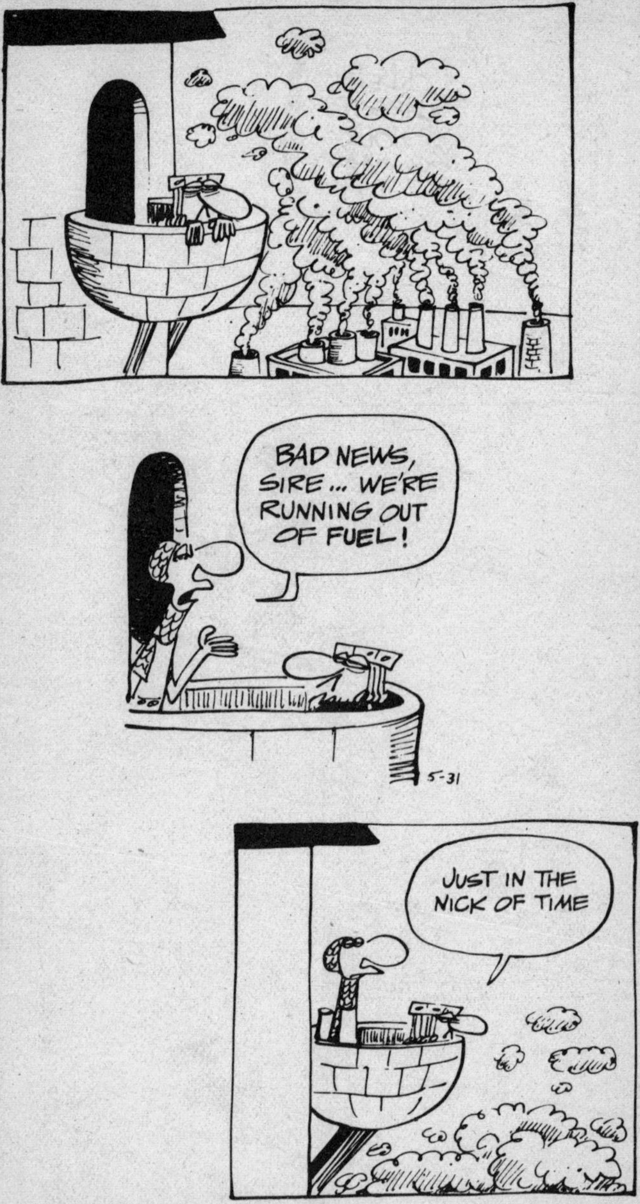
BAD NEWS, SIRE... WE'RE RUNNING OUT OF FUEL!
5-31
JUST IN THE NICK OF TIME

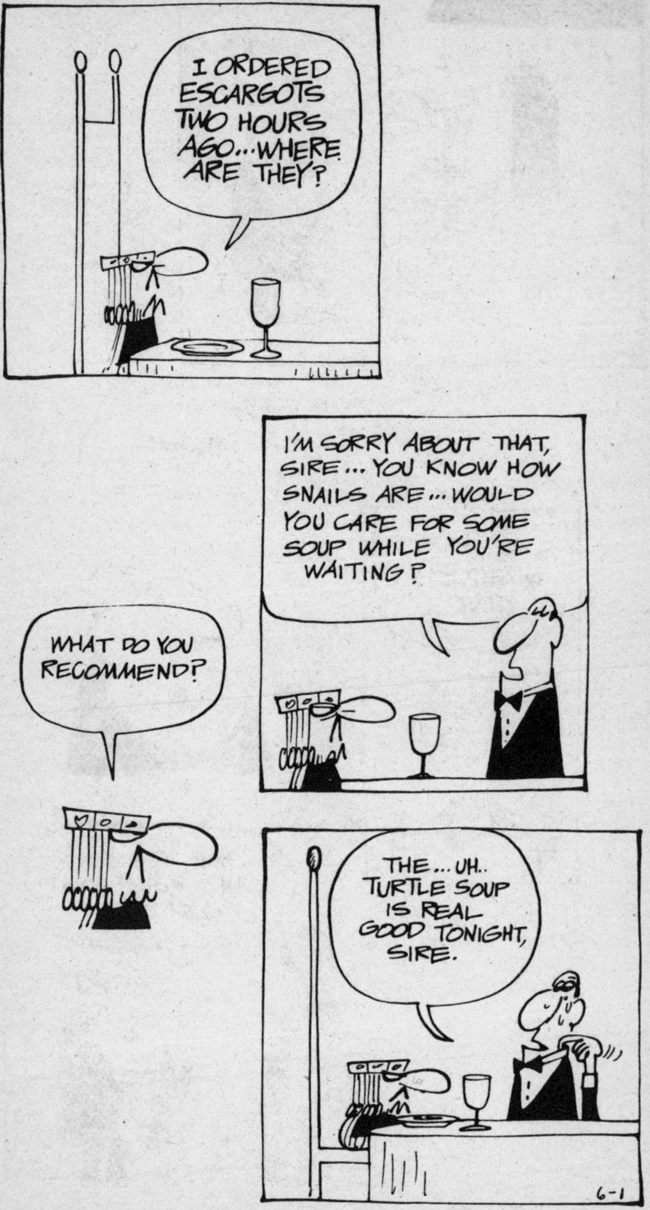
I ORDERED ESCARGOTS TWO HOURS AGO... WHERE ARE THEY?
I'M SORRY ABOUT THAT, SIRE... YOU KNOW HOW SNAILS ARE... WOULD YOU CARE FOR SOME SOUP WHILE YOU'RE WAITING?
WHAT DO YOU RECOMMEND?
THE... UH.. TURTLE SOUP IS REAL GOOD TONIGHT, SIRE.
6-1

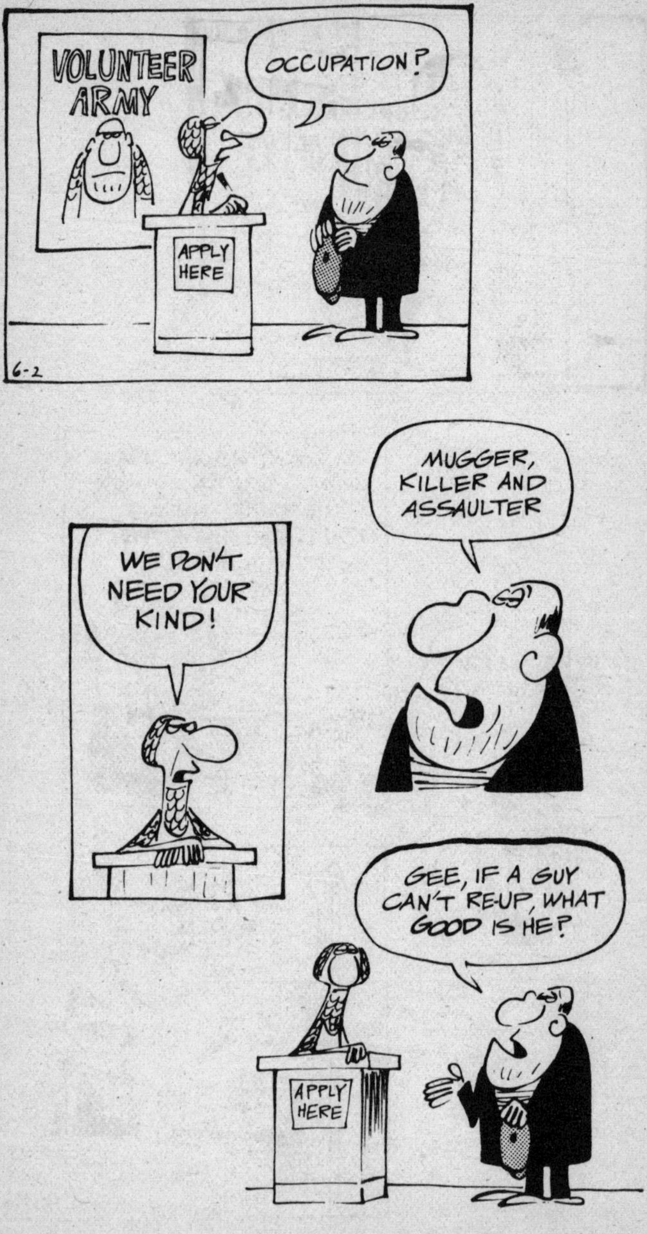
VOLUNTEER ARMY
OCCUPATION?
APPLY HERE
6-2
MUGGER, KILLER AND ASSAULTER
WE DON'T NEED YOUR KIND!
GEE, IF A GUY CAN'T RE-UP, WHAT GOOD IS HE?
APPLY HERE

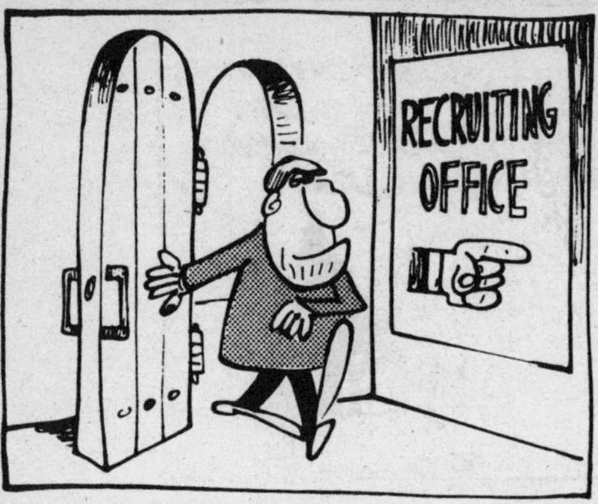
RECRUITING
OFFICE

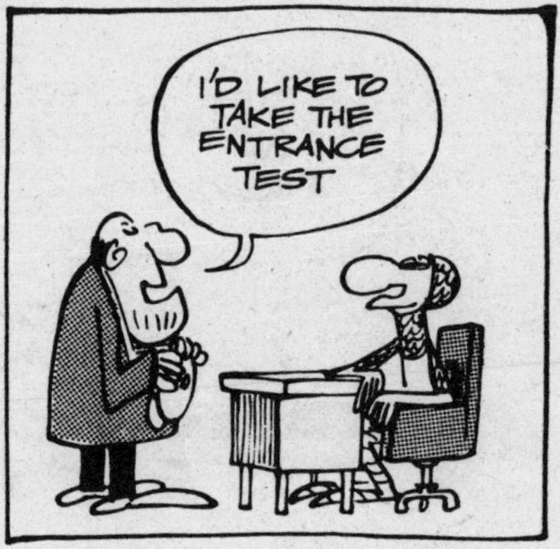
I'D LIKE TO TAKE THE ENTRANCE TEST

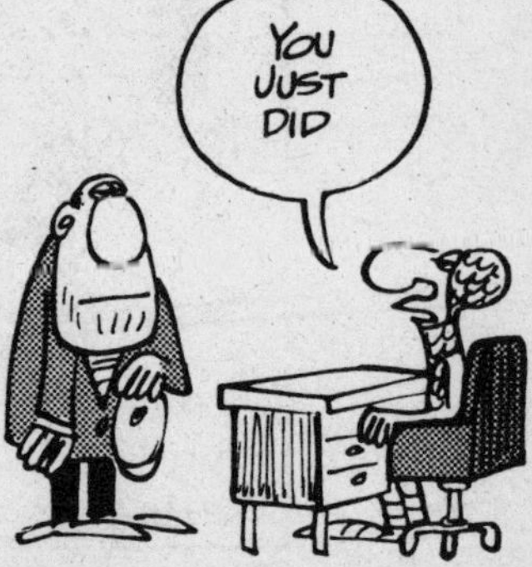
YOU JUST DID

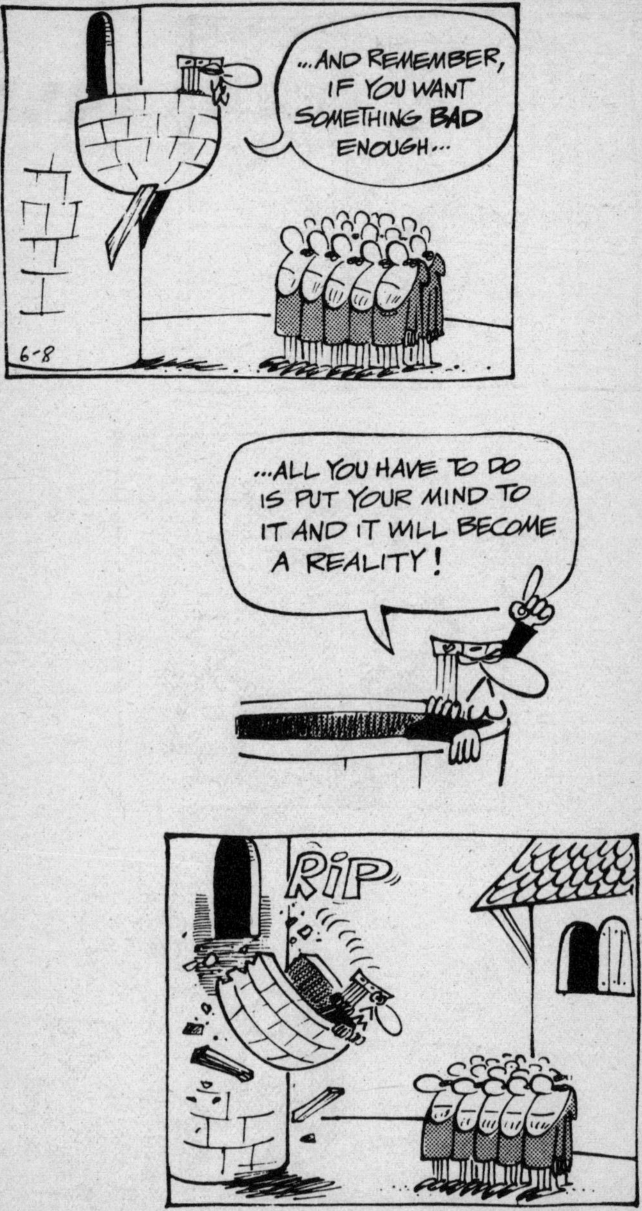
...AND REMEMBER, IF YOU WANT SOMETHING BAD ENOUGH...
6-8
...ALL YOU HAVE TO DO IS PUT YOUR MIND TO IT AND IT WILL BECOME A REALITY!
RIP

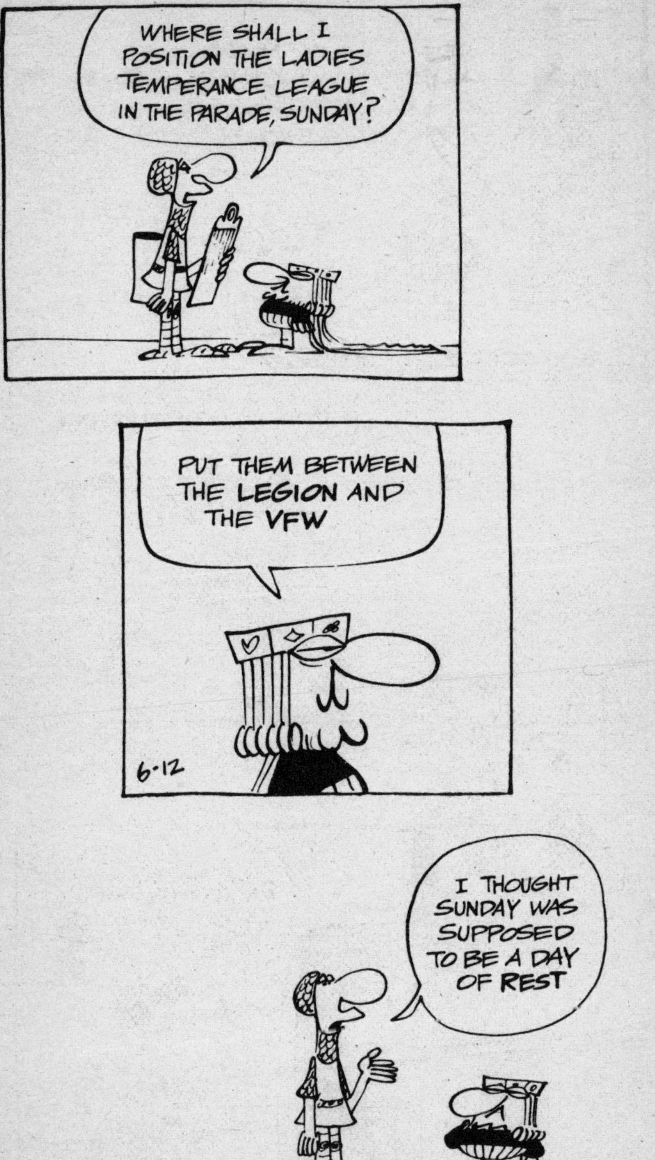
WHERE SHALL I POSITION THE LADIES TEMPERANCE LEAGUE IN THE PARADE, SUNDAY?
PUT THEM BETWEEN THE LEGION AND THE VFW
6-12
I THOUGHT SUNDAY WAS SUPPOSED TO BE A DAY OF REST

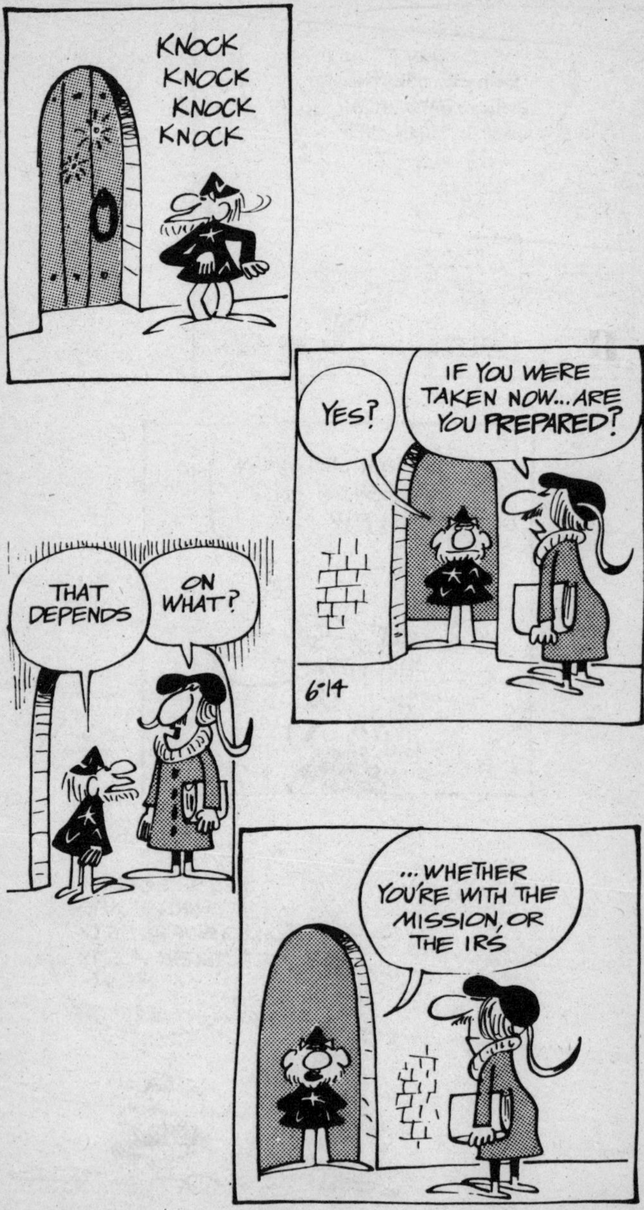
KNOCK KNOCK KNOCK KNOCK
YES?
IF YOU WERE TAKEN NOW...ARE YOU PREPARED?
6-14
THAT DEPENDS
ON WHAT?
...WHETHER YOU'RE WITH THE MISSION, OR THE IRS

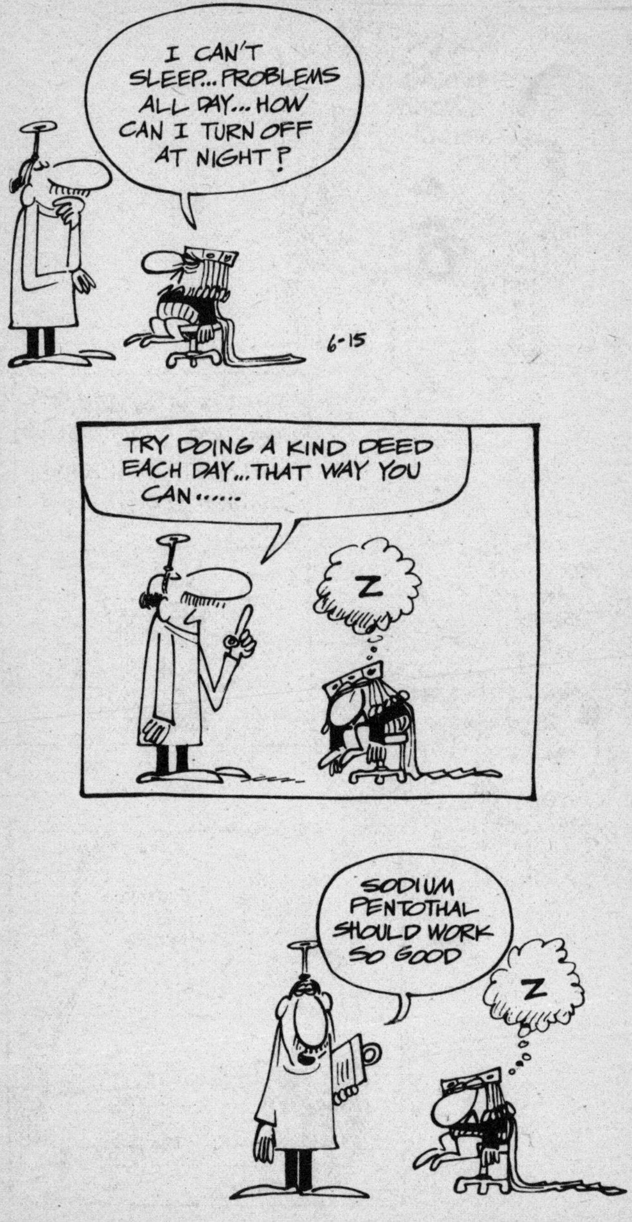
I CAN'T SLEEP... PROBLEMS ALL DAY... HOW CAN I TURN OFF AT NIGHT?
6-15
TRY DOING A KIND DEED EACH DAY... THAT WAY YOU CAN......
Z
SODIUM PENTOTHAL SHOULD WORK SO GOOD
Z

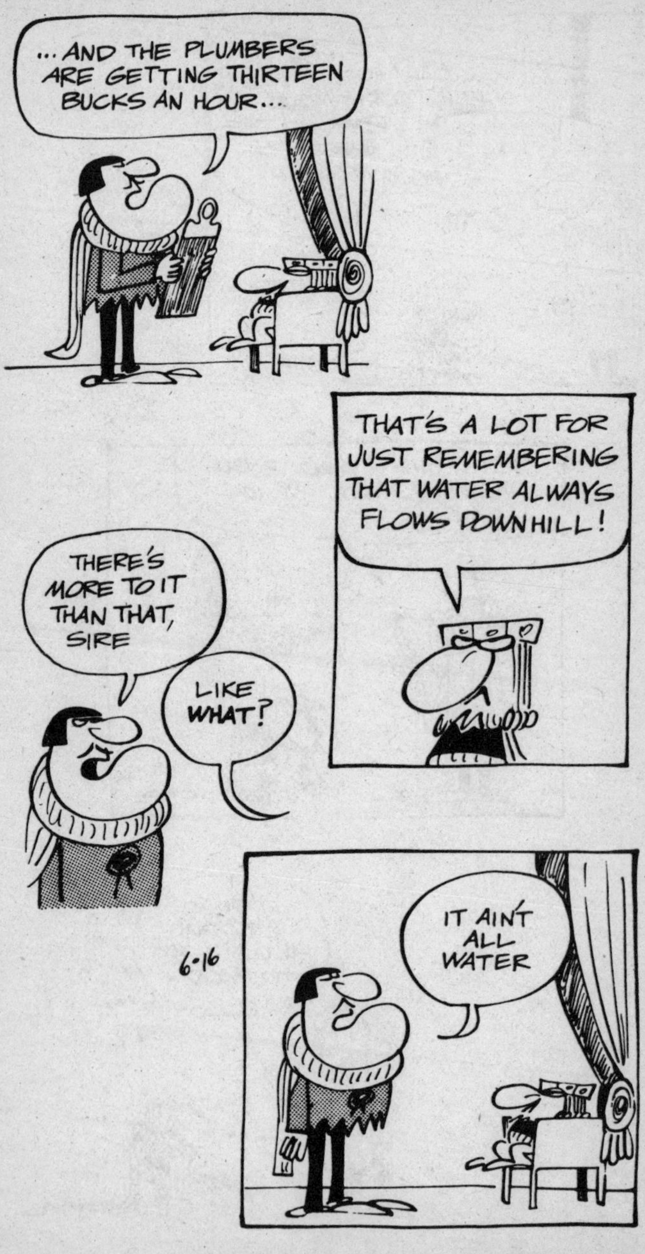
...AND THE PLUMBERS ARE GETTING THIRTEEN BUCKS AN HOUR...
THAT'S A LOT FOR JUST REMEMBERING THAT WATER ALWAYS FLOWS DOWNHILL!
THERE'S MORE TO IT THAN THAT, SIRE
LIKE WHAT?
IT AIN'T ALL WATER
6-16

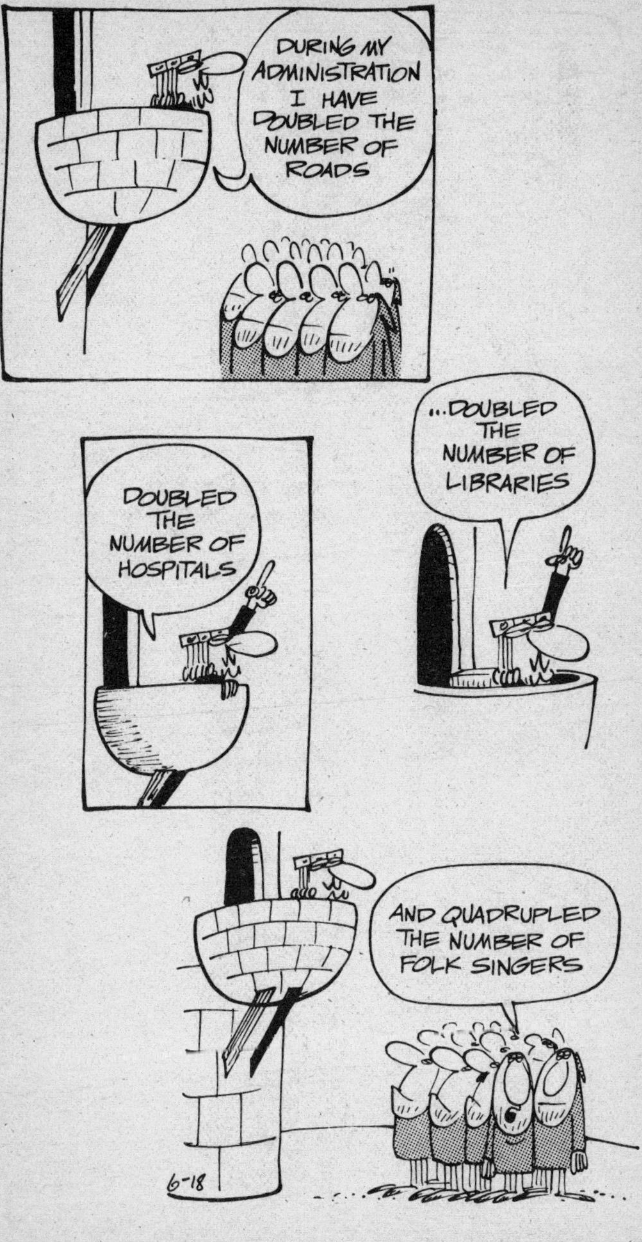
DURING MY ADMINISTRATION I HAVE DOUBLED THE NUMBER OF ROADS
DOUBLED THE NUMBER OF HOSPITALS
...DOUBLED THE NUMBER OF LIBRARIES
AND QUADRUPLED THE NUMBER OF FOLK SINGERS
6-18

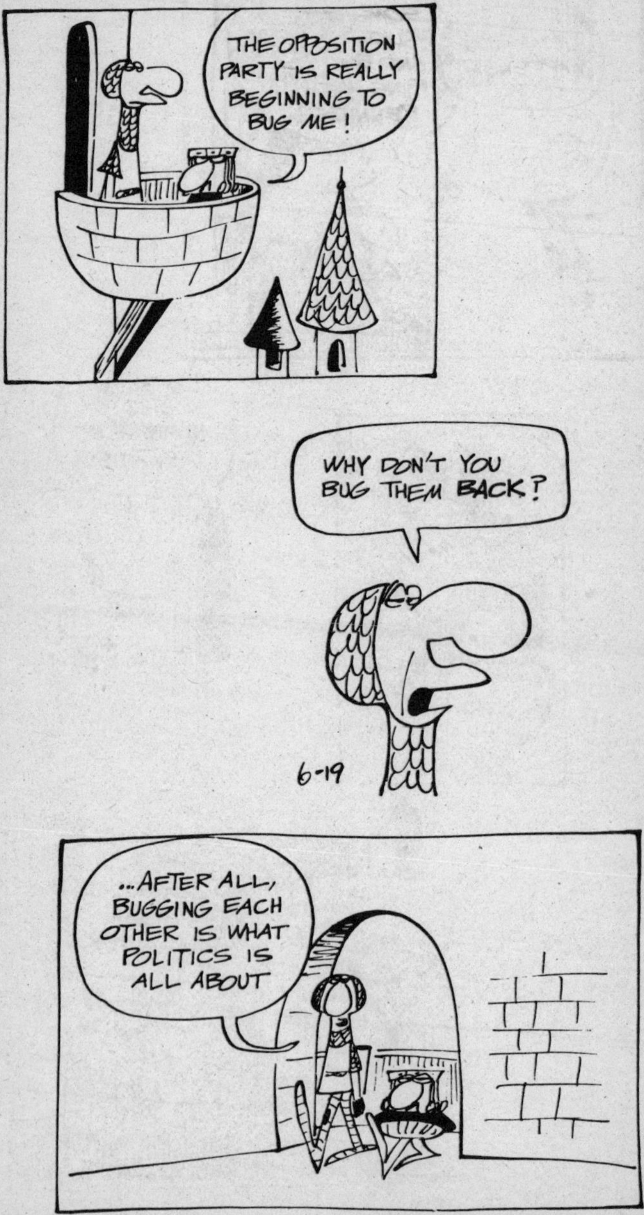
THE OPPOSITION PARTY IS REALLY BEGINNING TO BUG ME!
WHY DON'T YOU BUG THEM BACK?
6-19
...AFTER ALL, BUGGING EACH OTHER IS WHAT POLITICS IS ALL ABOUT

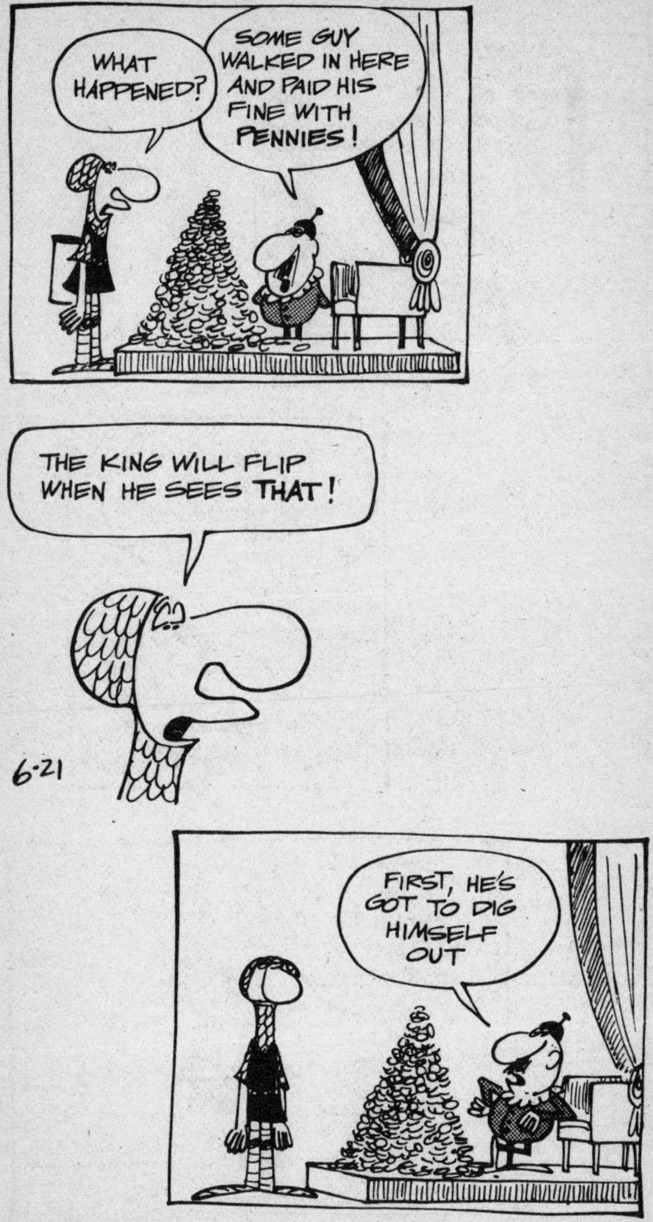
WHAT HAPPENED?
SOME GUY WALKED IN HERE AND PAID HIS FINE WITH PENNIES!
THE KING WILL FLIP WHEN HE SEES THAT!
6-21
FIRST, HE'S GOT TO DIG HIMSELF OUT

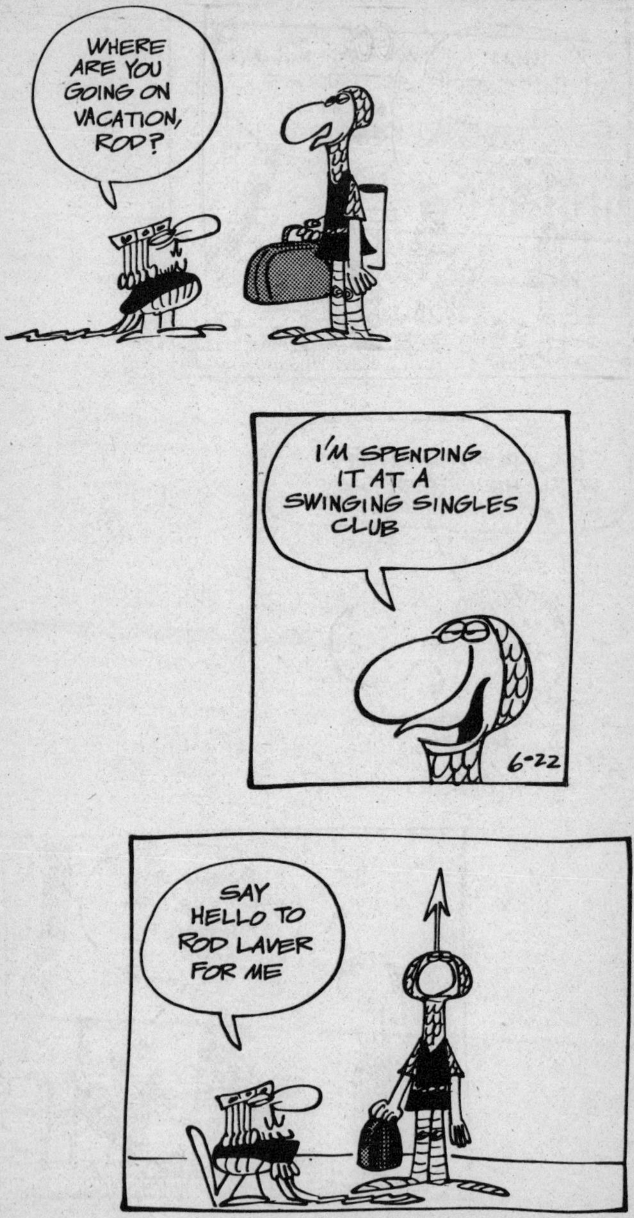
WHERE ARE YOU GOING ON VACATION, ROD?
I'M SPENDING IT AT A SWINGING SINGLES CLUB
6-22
SAY HELLO TO ROD LAVER FOR ME

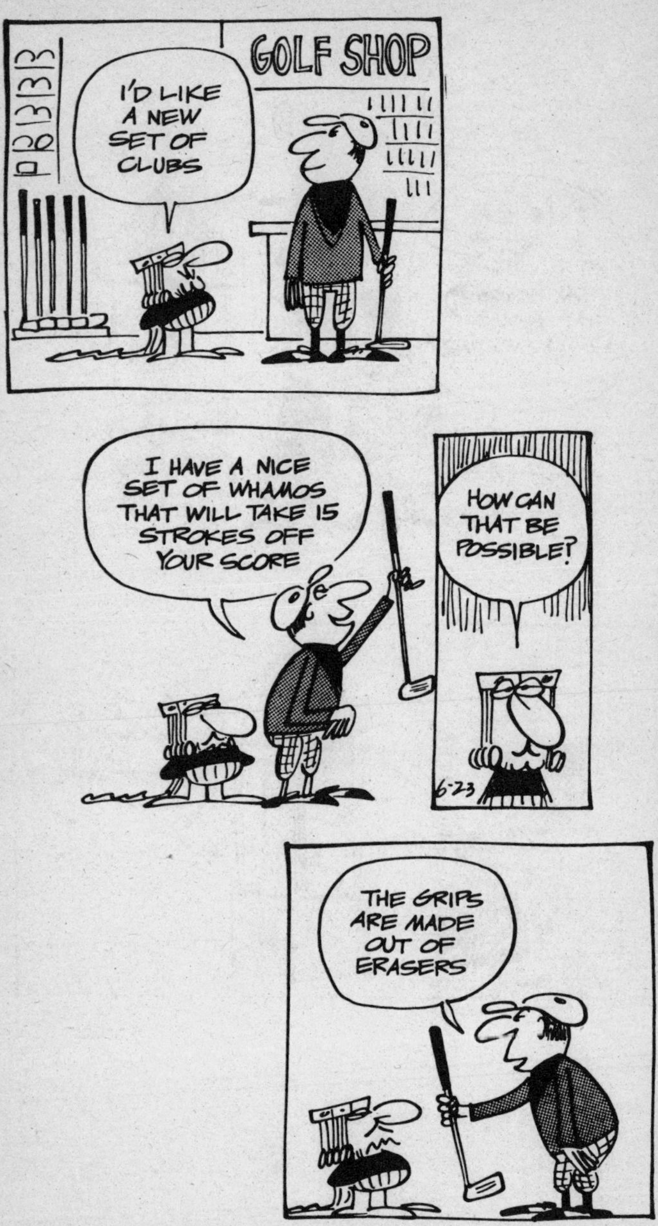
GOLF SHOP
I'D LIKE A NEW SET OF CLUBS
I HAVE A NICE SET OF WHAMOS THAT WILL TAKE 15 STROKES OFF YOUR SCORE
HOW CAN THAT BE POSSIBLE?
6-23
THE GRIPS ARE MADE OUT OF ERASERS

I AM HERE TO PROTEST MY CLIENT'S TAXATION WITHOUT REPRESENTATION!
GRIEVANCE DAYS
GRIEVANCE DAYS
YOUR CLIENT COULDN'T HAVE PICKED A BETTER MAN.
6·28

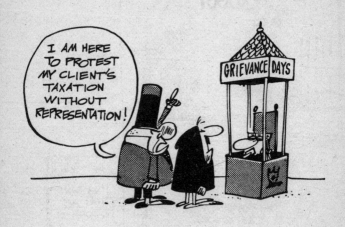

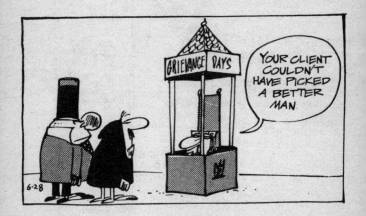

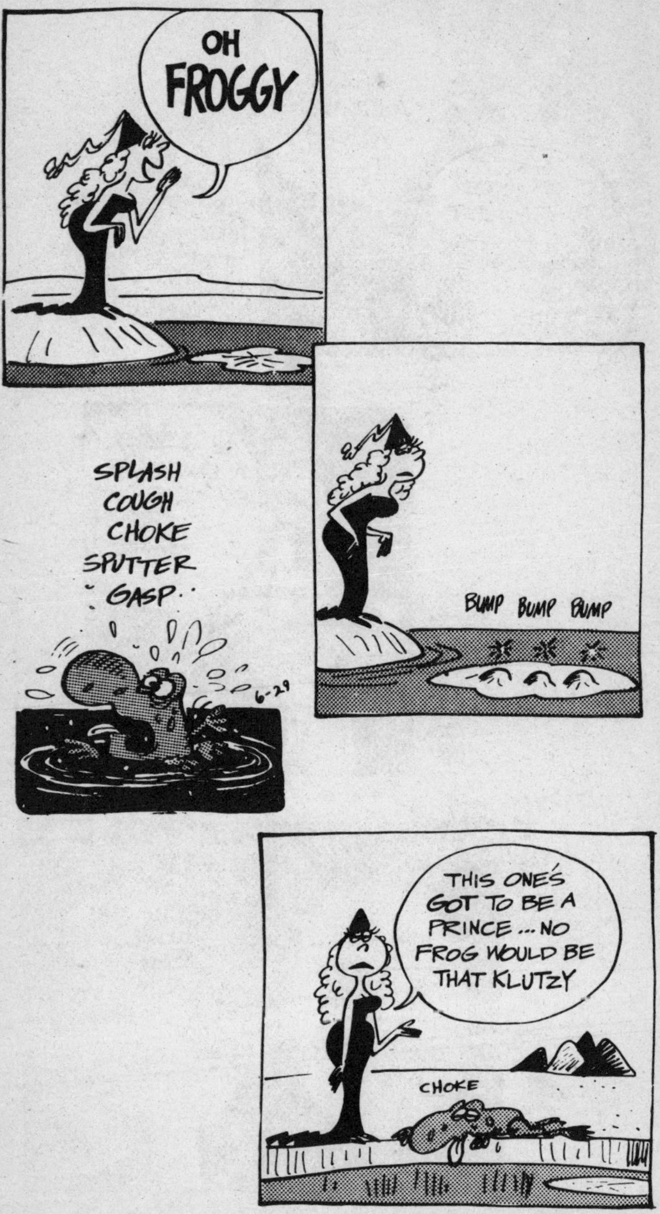
OH FROGGY
BUMP BUMP BUMP
SPLASH
COUGH
CHOKE
SPUTTER
GASP
6-29
THIS ONE'S GOT TO BE A PRINCE ... NO FROG WOULD BE THAT KLUTZY
CHOKE

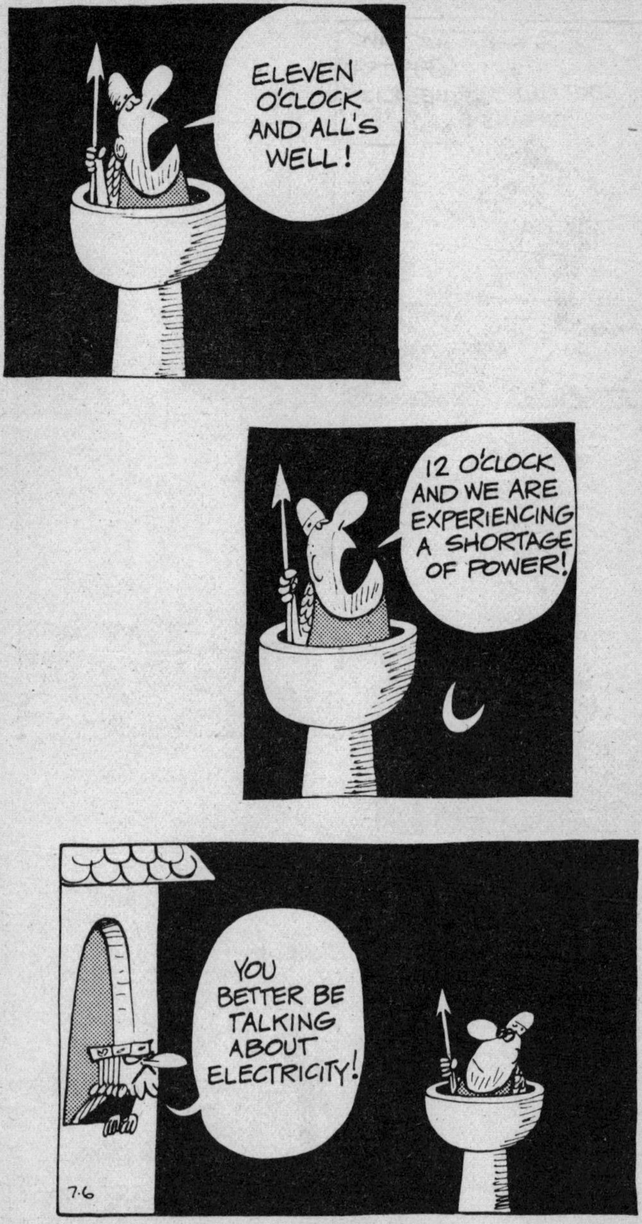

ELEVEN O'CLOCK AND ALL'S WELL!
12 O'CLOCK AND WE ARE EXPERIENCING A SHORTAGE OF POWER!
YOU BETTER BE TALKING ABOUT ELECTRICITY!
7·6

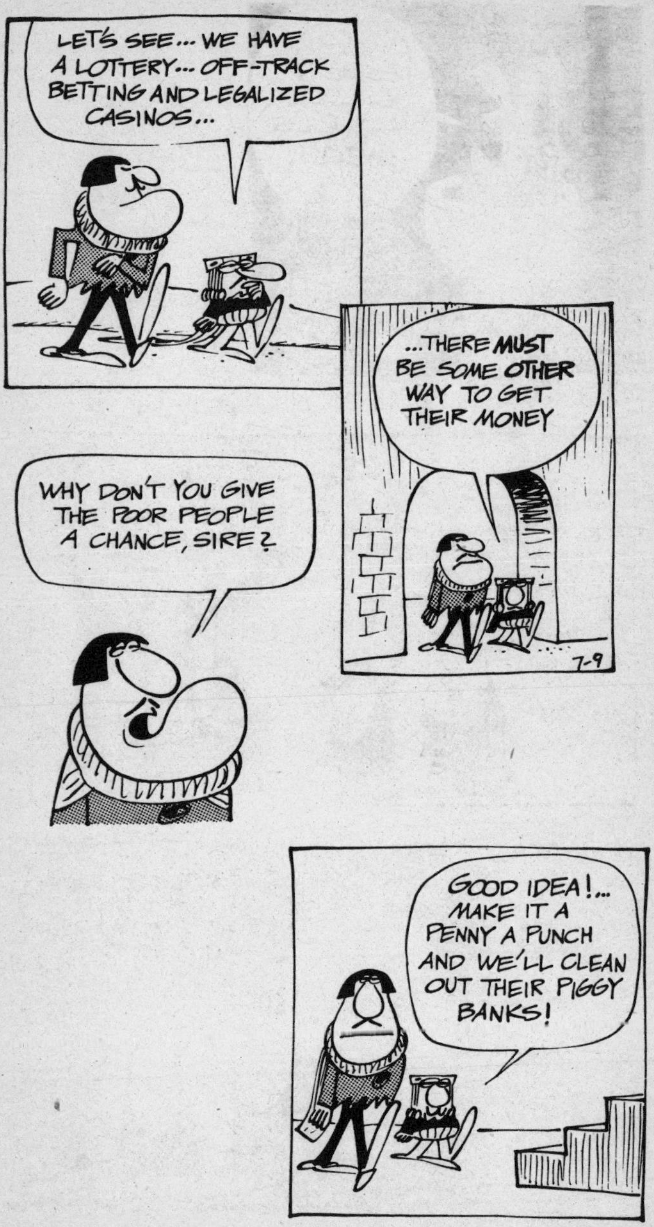
LET'S SEE... WE HAVE A LOTTERY... OFF-TRACK BETTING AND LEGALIZED CASINOS...
...THERE MUST BE SOME OTHER WAY TO GET THEIR MONEY
7-9
WHY DON'T YOU GIVE THE POOR PEOPLE A CHANCE, SIRE?
GOOD IDEA!... MAKE IT A PENNY A PUNCH AND WE'LL CLEAN OUT THEIR PIGGY BANKS!

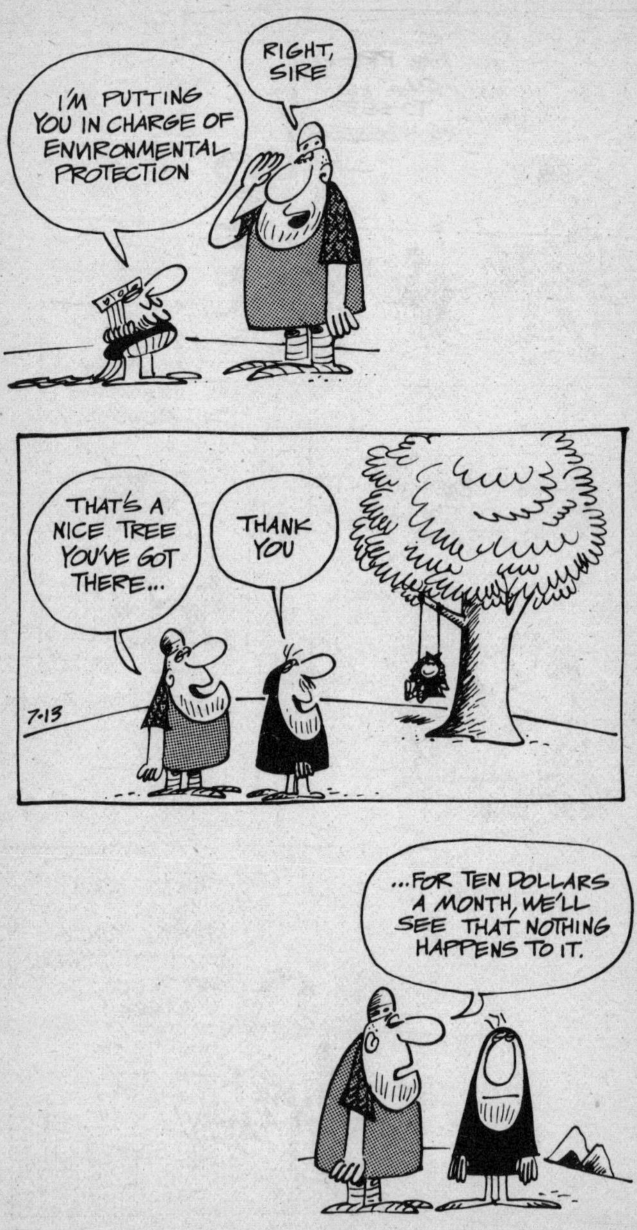
I'M PUTTING YOU IN CHARGE OF ENVIRONMENTAL PROTECTION
RIGHT, SIRE
THAT'S A NICE TREE YOU'VE GOT THERE...
THANK YOU
7-13
...FOR TEN DOLLARS A MONTH, WE'LL SEE THAT NOTHING HAPPENS TO IT.

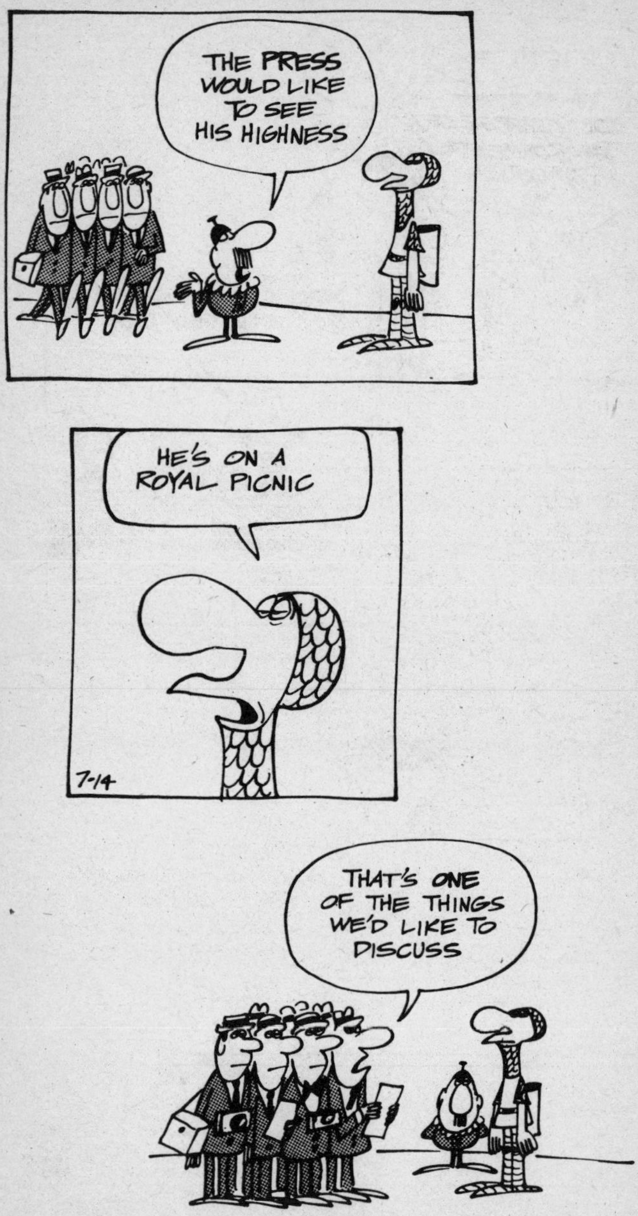
THE PRESS WOULD LIKE TO SEE HIS HIGHNESS
HE'S ON A ROYAL PICNIC
7-14
THAT'S ONE OF THE THINGS WE'D LIKE TO DISCUSS

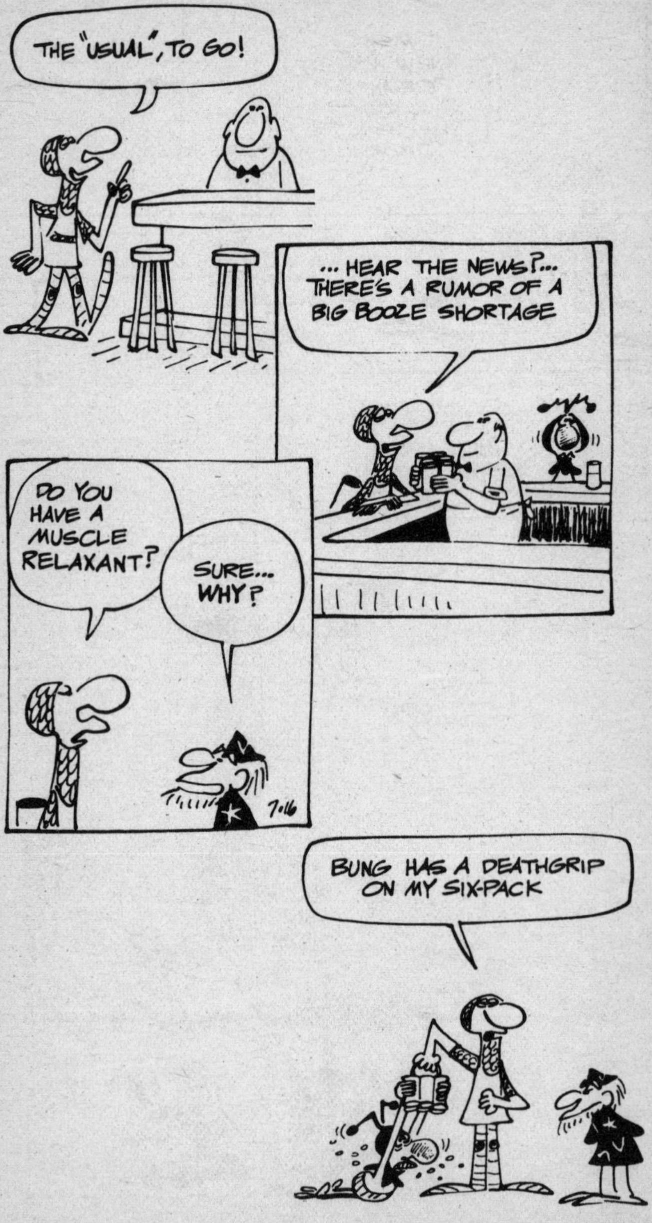
THE "USUAL", TO GO!
... HEAR THE NEWS?... THERE'S A RUMOR OF A BIG BOOZE SHORTAGE
DO YOU HAVE A MUSCLE RELAXANT?
SURE... WHY?
7-16
BUNG HAS A DEATHGRIP ON MY SIX-PACK

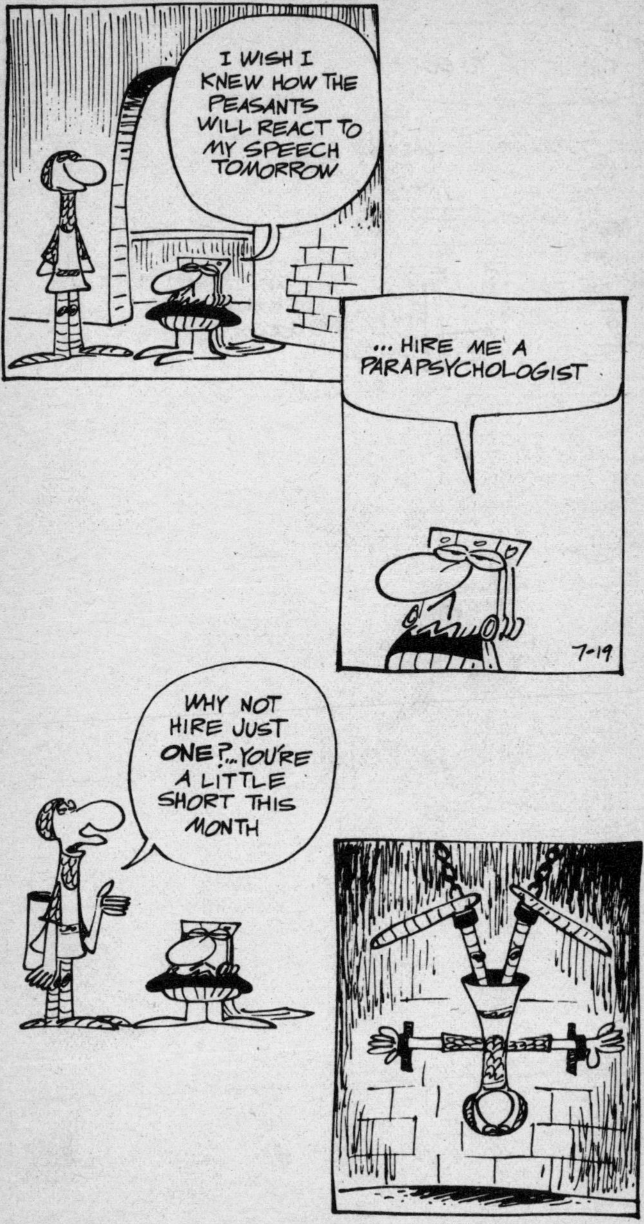
I WISH I KNEW HOW THE PEASANTS WILL REACT TO MY SPEECH TOMORROW
... HIRE ME A PARAPSYCHOLOGIST
7-19
WHY NOT HIRE JUST ONE?...YOU'RE A LITTLE SHORT THIS MONTH

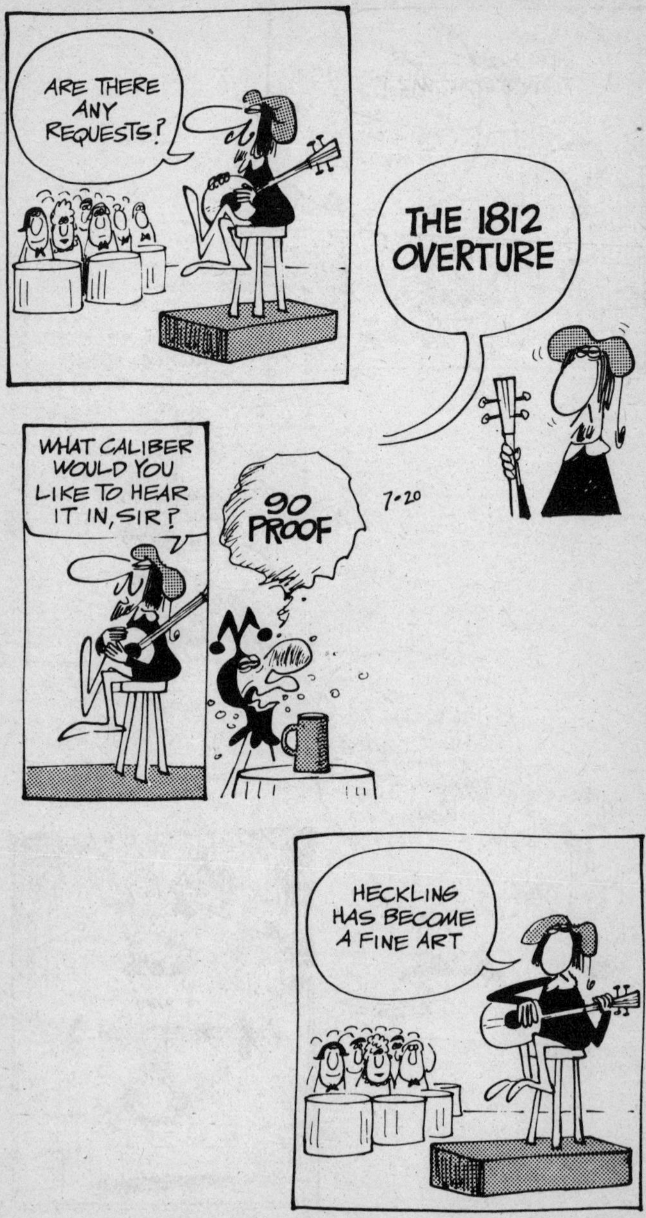

ARE THERE ANY REQUESTS?
THE 1812 OVERTURE
WHAT CALIBER WOULD YOU LIKE TO HEAR IT IN, SIR?
90 PROOF
7-20
HECKLING HAS BECOME A FINE ART

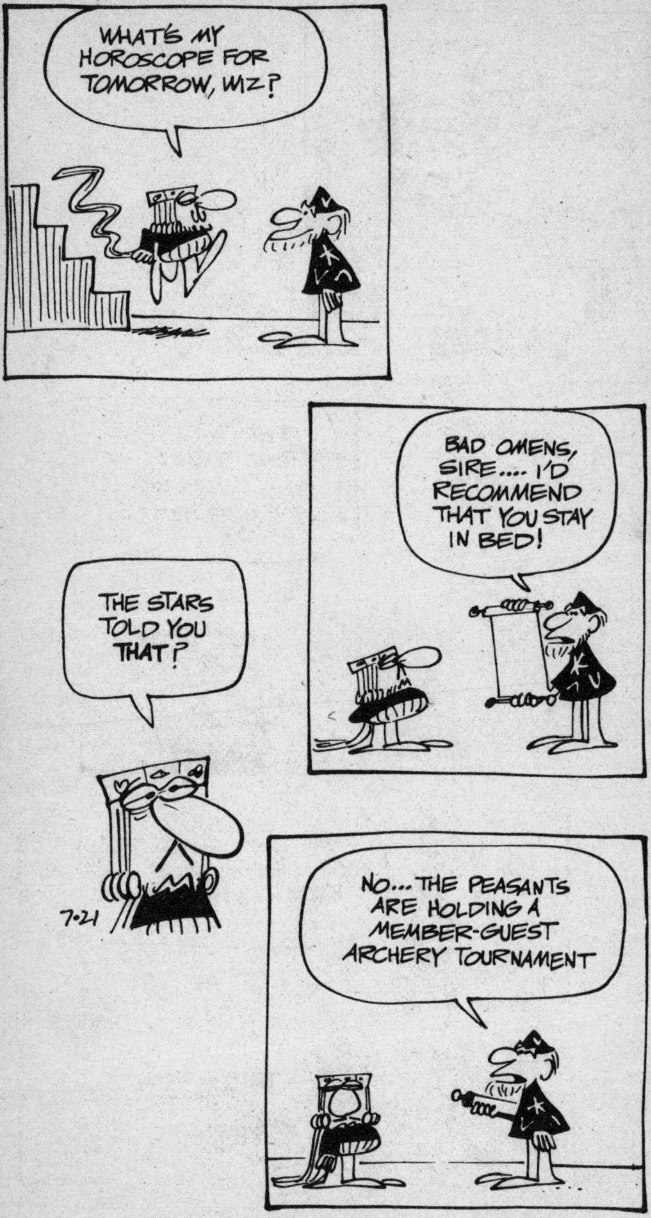
WHAT'S MY HOROSCOPE FOR TOMORROW, WIZ?
BAD OMENS, SIRE.... I'D RECOMMEND THAT YOU STAY IN BED!
THE STARS TOLD YOU THAT?
NO... THE PEASANTS ARE HOLDING A MEMBER-GUEST ARCHERY TOURNAMENT
7-21

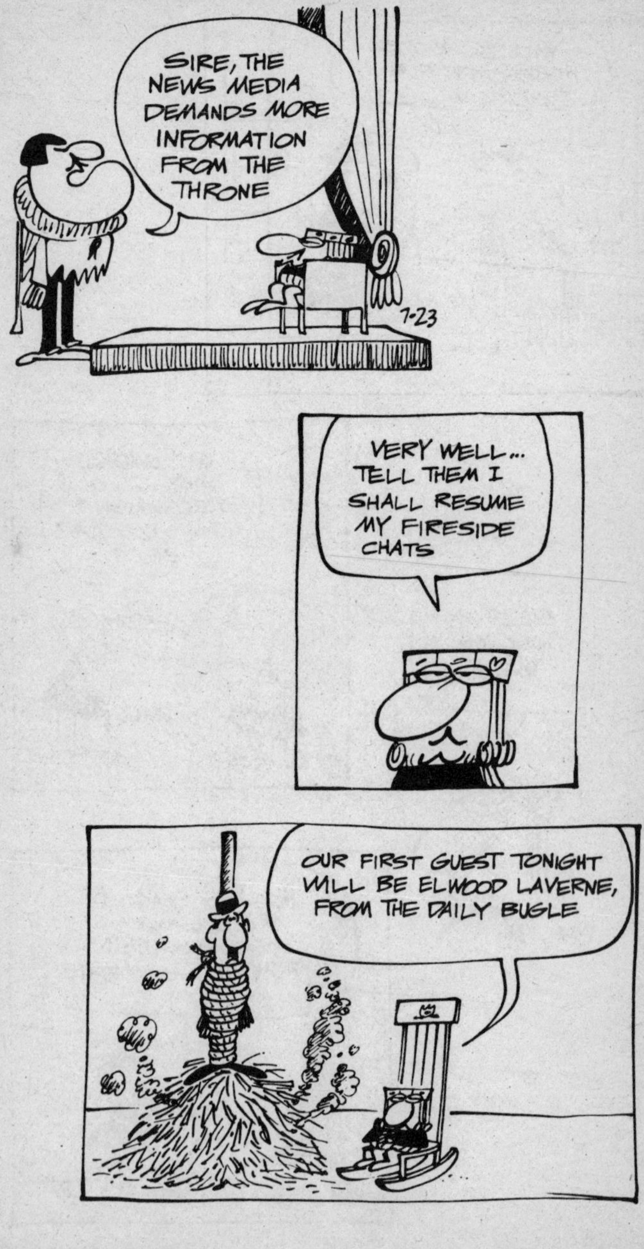
SIRE, THE NEWS MEDIA DEMANDS MORE INFORMATION FROM THE THRONE
7-23
VERY WELL... TELL THEM I SHALL RESUME MY FIRESIDE CHATS
OUR FIRST GUEST TONIGHT WILL BE ELWOOD LAVERNE, FROM THE DAILY BUGLE

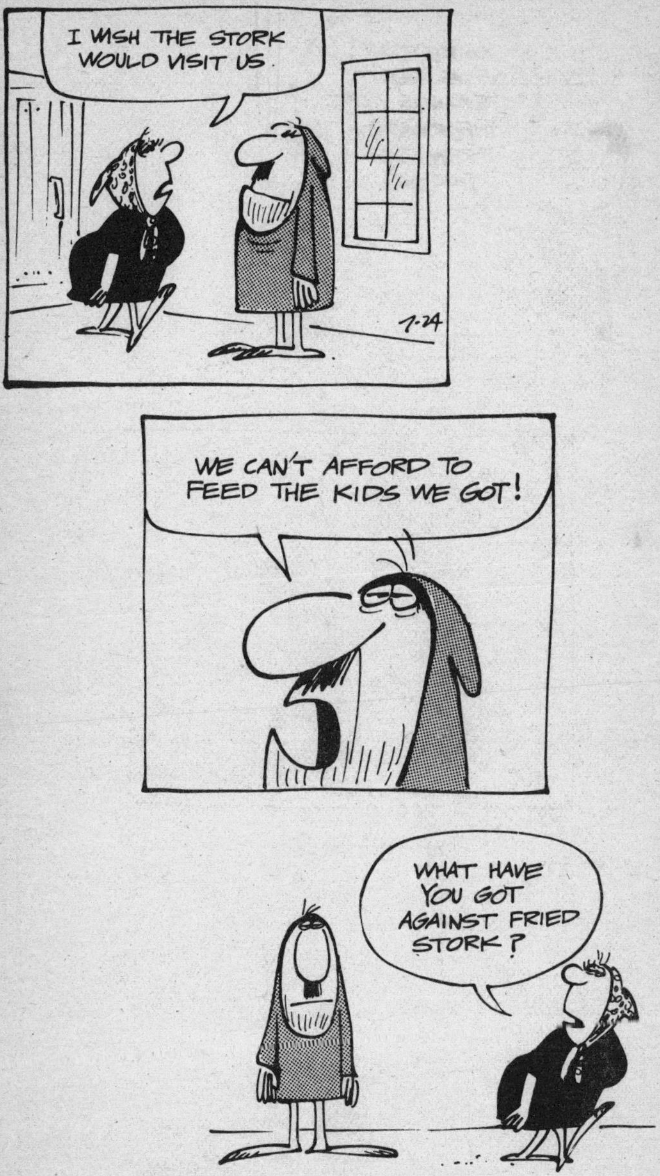
I WISH THE STORK WOULD VISIT US.
1-24
WE CAN'T AFFORD TO FEED THE KIDS WE GOT!
WHAT HAVE YOU GOT AGAINST FRIED STORK?

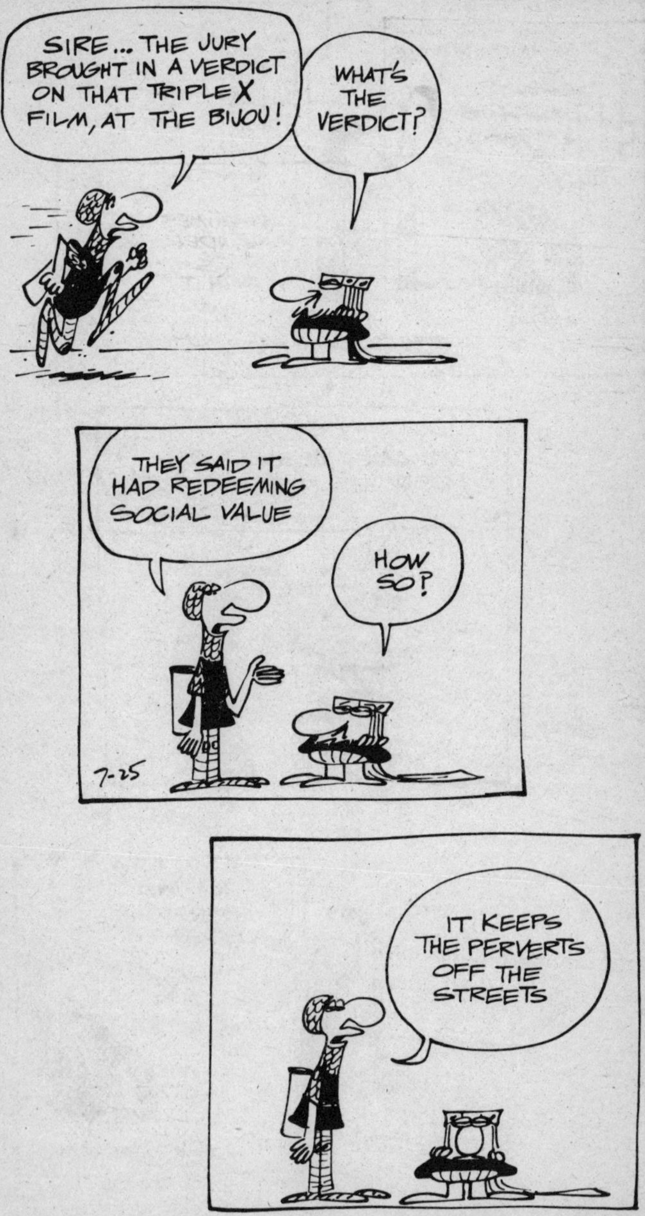
SIRE... THE JURY BROUGHT IN A VERDICT ON THAT TRIPLE X FILM, AT THE BIJOU!
WHAT'S THE VERDICT?
THEY SAID IT HAD REDEEMING SOCIAL VALUE
HOW SO?
7-25
IT KEEPS THE PERVERTS OFF THE STREETS

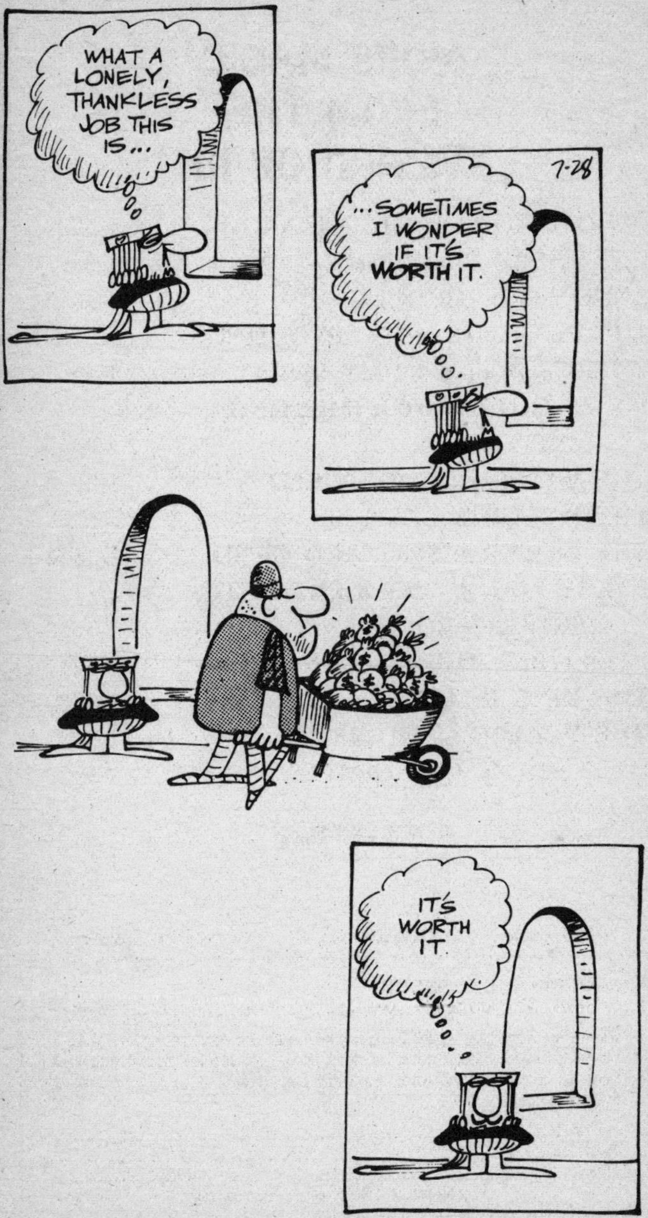
WHAT A LONELY, THANKLESS JOB THIS IS...
7-28
...SOMETIMES I WONDER IF IT'S WORTH IT.
IT'S WORTH IT.

MORE MAGIC
FROM THE
WIZARD OF ID

I'M OFF TO SEE THE WIZARD	1-3700-7
LET THERE BE REIGN	1-3892-5
LONG LIVE THE KING	1-3655-8
THE PEASANTS ARE REVOLTING	1-3671-X
THERE'S A FLY IN MY SWILL	1-3687-6
WE'VE GOT TO STOP MEETING LIKE THIS	1-3633-7
THE WIZARD OF ID—YIELD	1-3653-1
THE WIZARD'S BACK	1-3654-X
THE WONDROUS WIZARD OF ID	1-3648-5
EVERY MAN IS INNOCENT UNTIL PROVEN BROKE	1-3650-7
REMEMBER THE GOLDEN RULE	1-3717-1
THE KING IS A FINK	1-3709-0
THE WIZARD OF ID #8	1-3681-7
HELP STAMP OUT GRAPES	1-3992-1

$1.25 Each

Buy them at your local bookstores or use this handy coupon for ordering:

FAWCETT BOOKS GROUP
P.O. Box C730, 524 Myrtle Ave., Pratt Station, Brooklyn, N.Y. 11205

Please send me the books I have checked above. Orders for less than 5 books must include 75¢ for the first book and 25¢ for each additional book to cover mailing and handling. I enclose $_____ in check or money order.

Name_____

Address_____

City_____ State/Zip_____

Please allow 4 to 5 weeks for delivery.